From the

SOPHENE

Published by Sophene 2023

The *History of the Vartanants Saints* by Yeghishe was
translated into English by Beyon Miloyan in 2023.
This edition is Volume I of II.

www.sophenebooks.com
www.sophenearmenianlibrary.com

ISBN-13: 978-1-925937-86-2

ԵՂԻՇԷԻ

ՊԱՏՄՈՒԹԻՒՆ ՍՐԲՈՑՆ ՎԱՐԴԱՆԱՆՑՆ

ՀԱՏՈՐ Ա.

ՏՊԱՐԱՆ
ԾՈՓՔ
Լոս Անճելըս

YEGHISHE

HISTORY
OF THE
VARTANANTS SAINTS

IN TWO VOLUMES OF CLASSICAL ARMENIAN
WITH AN ENGLISH TRANSLATION BY
BEYON MILOYAN

VOLUME I

SOPHENE BOOKS
LOS ANGELES

To my beloved grandparents,
Noubar and Marie Agopian.

GLOSSARY

Avag (*աւագ*) refers to a chief, noble or senior official.

Avan (*աւան*) refers to a village, town or district.

Azat (*ազատ*), a member of the Armenian nobility (lit. free), ranking below nakharars.

Dahekan (*դահեկան*) refers to a unit of mass probably equivalent to about 5 grams, or to such coinage.

Darandardzapet (*դարանդարձապետ*), a Sasanian chancellor or high-ranking legal official.

Dev (*դեւ*) refers to good or evil spirits.

Hazarbed (*հազարապետ*), a high official of the Sasanian state, lit. chief of a thousand (but see "hazarbed" in Encylopedia Iranica).

Magus (*մոգ*), a Zoroastrian priest.

Marzban (*մարզպան*), a Sasanian administrative title that refers to a governor or military commander of a border province.

Mogbed (*մոգպետ*), a high-ranking magus.

Movpetan Movpet (*մովպետան մովպետ*), the highest-ranking mogbed.

Nakharar (*նախարար*), a hereditary class of Armenian feudal lords and the highest ranking nobles (see "Naxarar" in the Encyclopedia Iranica).

Pshtipan (փշտիպան), bodyguard.

Sepuh (*սեպուհ*), a junior class of Armenian nobility.

Sparapet (*սպարապետ*), the commander-in-chief of the Armenian army (hereditary).

Vardapet (*վարդապետ*), a high-ranking and learned member of Armenian clergy, similar to the Orthodox archimandrite.

TRANSLATOR'S PREFACE

The *History of the Vartanants Saints* is a major source for the Battle of Avarayr, its causes and aftermath. The History covers the thirty-six-year period from AD 428 to 464 in seven chapters. Volume I contains the first four chapters and covers the period from the fall of the Armenian Arsacid dynasty (428 AD) to the events that led to the Battle of Avarayr (451). Volume II covers the period from the Battle of Avarayr to its aftermath in 464. But Yeghishe's *History* is otherwise an account of the Vartanants and Ghevontiants saints who were martyred in the war.

Volume I was initially published under the title *History of Vartan and the Armenian War* («Վասն Վարդանայ եւ Հայոց Պատերազմին»), first ascribed to the book by the Mkhitarist Fathers in the 19th century, and later popularized by Ter-Minasyan's 1957 critical edition.[1] With the completion of Volume II, I amended the title of my translation to the *History of the Vartanants Saints* («Պատմութիւն Սրբոցն Վարդանանցն»), the earliest known title of the book as recorded in Kirakos Gandzakets'i's *History of the Armenians*.[2] This change is not merely a reversion to an earlier title, but also an attempt to capture the spirit of the book more accurately, as Yeghishe was, in the first instance, writing a history, martyrology and panegyric of saints. Thus, whereas only a few pages of the book deal with the Battle of Avarayr, pages upon pages are devoted to portraying saintly acts of virtue, both individual and collective. This is not to downplay the political and military aspects of Yeghishe's *History*, but to emphasize that the distinguishing feature of Yeghishe's collective(s)—be it the nation, its soldiers, princes or clergy—is that they are composed of individuals united by covenant (*ուխտ*) in a spirit of Christian brotherhood, and not merely on the basis of secular-national bonds.

Little is known about the life of Yeghishe, though a corpus of works attributed to him has survived. Only some of these bear the same distinct style in which the *History of the Vartanants Saints* was composed.[3] His elaborate prose and profound theology indicate he was a *vartabed*, and perhaps also a bishop, and his essay on monastic life indicates that he joined the cloister, probably later in life. There is one reference in our *History* to a Yeghisha, bishop of Amatunik,[a] which Yeghishe does not identify as himself but which some readers have surmised to be a reference to our author. If true, then Yeghishe would have been an eyewitness of the events he was reporting as he himself states in three instances:

> *"Behold, it is not willingly that we describe, with tearful laments, the many blows we received and that we were eyewitness to."*[b]

> *"I myself happened to be there and saw and heard the sound of [the king's] impudent voice."*[c]

> *"As we saw at this time with our own eyes, the same nahatakutyun took place in Armenia."*[d]

Despite these claims, there has been considerable debate about whether Yeghishe was, in fact, a contemporary historian. Though I believe the debate is a moot one, as we cannot rule out that Yeghishe was a contemporary, I briefly address it here. While the earliest known reference to Yeghishe in Armenian literature is by the 10th century historian, Tovma Artsruni, according to whom Yeghishe had been Saint Vartan's scribe, it was not until the 19th century that Yeghishe's status as a contemporary was first called into question, beginning with a series of three articles by Ter-Poghosyan in the 1895 issues of *Handes Amsorya*.[4]

a Vol. I, p. 55

b Vol. I, p. 7

c Vol. I, p. 29

d Vol. II, p. 2

Ter-Poghosyan concluded, based on a comparison of several excerpts from Yeghishe's and Ghazar's histories, that despite Yeghishe's claims of being an eyewitness, it was likelier that he had relied on Ghazar's account than vice versa. Now because Ghazar, about whom we have more biographical information, is known to be a later author (as his *History* covers the period 387-485), Ter-Poghosyan implies that Yeghishe was at least a 6th century author. This view was most recently popularized by Robert Thomson,[5] who based his own judgment on a comparison of the original historical information conveyed in the two works, observing that there are only minor differences between them. While these speculations have been fueled by the fact that neither author mentions the other, Ter-Poghosyan's and Thomson's arguments both hinge on the point that Yeghishe's mere claims to being an eyewitness do not amount to solid evidence, and thus we are to treat these as literary embellishments intended to add gravitas to his work.

However Yeghishe's status as an eyewitness is not confined to these two claims, as we see in the following examples:

> *"But although we are not permitted to speak against the ruler [Yazdegerd II], neither can we praise a man who will fight against God."*[e]

> *"This blessed Khuzhik [...] repeated to us in order what took place [...]."*[f]

> *"Yet I cannot count the numbers of the blessed wives of the valiant ones or the prisoners and casualties of the war throughout Armenia because there are many more whom I do not know about than those I do. For there are about five hundred whom I recognize personally, not restricted to the senior ranks, but also many among the junior ranks."*[g]

---

e Vol. I, p. 29.

f Vol II, p. 197.

g Vol. II, p. 237.

The second point may also be viewed by skeptics as support for the notion that Yeghishe copied from Ghazar, as Ghazar recalls the same Khuzhik as an informant ("*...as was accurately learned from the blessed Khuzhik...*" *[Vol. I, p. 287]*),[6] though his later date of authorship makes his having a direct informant unlikely. However, these similarities need not imply that one copied from the other. As Ter-Poghosyan first observed, overlaps between the two works can also be explained by their reliance on common sources. But it should be emphasized that this would not rule out Yeghishe's status as a contemporary (as Ter-Poghosyan went on to claim) inasmuch as a contemporary would be expected to use reference material.

But what these debates have failed to mention is that both Yeghishe and Ghazar had Mamikonian patrons, thus raising the question: If Yeghishe was in fact a later author who copied from Ghazar, was his Mamikonian patron, David, unaware of it? Or should we assume that he instructed Yeghishe to base a whole new history on one part of Ghazar's narrative without a single reference to his *History*? Otherwise, are we to treat Yeghishe's claim to having a Mamikonian patron as yet another fabrication? I do not find these arguments convincing. While it is likely that both Yeghishe and Ghazar shared certain sources, Yeghishe's date of authorship will probably never be verified. Therefore, I am inclined to take Yeghishe at his word.

A final point on this topic is that Yeghishe's *History* does not only overlap with Ghazar's; for example, Yeghishe's account of King Vache of Aghuank's rebellion against Peroz[h] appears almost verbatim in Movses Dasxurants'i's *History of the Aghuans*,[i] which is known to be a later work.[7] To those who question Yeghishe's status as a contemporary, this may be taken to imply that Yeghishe was writing at least after the 7th century, as Nerses Akinean argued (though Akinean was making a more tenuous argument that Yeghishe was not even writing

h Vol II, p. 231.

i *History of the Aghuans,* Book I, p. 31.

about Avarayr).

Yeghishe makes one explicit literary reference in his entire work, and that is to the books of the Maccabees. From these books he appears to have borrowed concepts related to martyrdom and holy war that are so central to his own *History*, as well as certain imagery from its Armenian translation.[8] If we take Yeghishe at his word, then the Armenian translation of the Maccabees was already in circulation by the early 5th century, for as he says of St. Vartan, *"having been versed in Holy Scripture from childhood, he took hold of the brave description of the Maccabees and related their proceedings with exuberant words".*[j] The prominent Maccabean influence on Yeghishe's text, together with other aspects of his work, such as the saints' joyful acceptance of their persecutions and tortures, each individual's considering himself a martyr shrine[k], the emphasis on collecting the saints' relics[l] and establishing memorials in their names[m] are all characteristic of the so-called cult of the saints that was prominent in the 4th-6th century Near East.[9-11] St. Gregory Nazianzen, for example, had begun his homily on the Maccabean martyrs by asking his audience to consider what more the admirable Maccabees might have achieved had they had the benefit of emulating Christ's example. I believe Yeghishe's *History* can be viewed as a response to this question with the example of the Vartanants saints.

The 12th century Catholicos Saint Nerses Shnorhali drew on this same parallel between the Vartanants saints and the Maccabean martyrs in Chapter 6 of his *Lament on [the Fall of] Edessa* («*Ողբ Եդեսիոյ*»), linking, for the first time, the saints' martyrdom to Armenian national identity:

---

j Vol II, p. 19; according to Koriwn, also, Sahak had been an instructor to the Mamikonians, and to Vartan in particular.

k Vol. I, p. 27.

l Vol. II, p. 141, 191, 197.

m Vol II, p. 245.

Մակաբայեանց նմանէին եւ Վարդանանց պատերազմին,
Միշտ առ միմեանս ձայնէին, աղաղակաւ զայս ասէին.
Մի՛ երկիցուք զանգիտելով, եղբա՛րք, ի սրոյ մահկանացուին
Եւ ընդ քաջացն արիութիւն մի՛ խառնեցուք զերկիւղ վատին.
Անուն բարեաց ժառանգեցուք, որ ընթանայ յազգ երկրածին։

The Vartanantz martyrs like the Maccabees entered the fray
Cried out to one another—'Pray!
Fear not the mortal sword, brothers, do not dismay.
Dilute not the force of your brave valor as cowards—ne'er stray;
And bequeath your good name to our nation to stay.'

By the 19th century, Yeghishe's *History* would take on a fully national significance as the Battle of Avarayr came to be seen as a formative moment in the development of a distinctly Armenian national culture. Yeghishe's *History* continues to hold great national significance today and remains a cornerstone of Armenian literature.

The present translation was made from the critical edition of the classical Armenian text by Ter-Minasyan[1] and uses a modification of the Library of Congress transliteration for Eastern Armenian without diacritical marks and with modern Western Armenian transliteration for notable names. For additional bibliography, see Archbishop Levon Zekiyan's *Ełišē as Witness of the Ecclesiology of the Early Armenian Church*,[12] Cyril Toumanoff's *Armenia and Georgia*,[13] and Michael Bonner's outstanding, comprehensive history of the Sasanian empire, *The Last Empire of Iran*.[14]

BIBLIOGRAPHY

1. Ter-Minasyan, E. (1957). *Egishei Vasn Vardanay ew Hayots' Paterazmin.* Erevan.
2. Gandzaketsi, K. (2022). *Kirakos Gandzakets'i's History of the Armenians* (R. Bedrosian, trans.). Sophene.
3. Yeghishe. (1838). *Matenagrutiwnk nakhneats: Srboy Horn Meroy Yeghishei Vardapeti matenagrutiwnk.* San Lazzaro.
4. Ter-Poghosyan, G. (1895). Yeghishei patmut'ean aghbiwry. *Handes Amsorya, 9,* 20-23.
   —*Handes Amsorya, 9,* 58-61.
   —*Handes Amsorya, 9,* 110-113.
5. Thomson, R. (1982). *Elishe's History of Vardan and the Armenian War.* Harvard University Press.
6. Parpec'i. G. (2021). *Ghazar Parpec'i's History of the Armenians* (R. Bedrosian, trans.). Sophene.
7. Dasxurants'i, M. (2020). *History of the Aghuans.* (R. Bedrosian, trans.). Sophene.
8. Hatsuni, V. (1896). *Khorhrdatsut'iwnk' yeghishei patmut'ean veray.* San Lazzaro.
9. Chrysostom, J. (2006). *The Cult of the Saints: Select Homilies and Letters* (W. Mayer, ed.). New York.
10. Brown, P. (2015). *The Cult of the Saints: Its Rise and Function in Latin Christianity* (2nd ed.). Chicago.
11. Howard-Johnston, J., & Hayward, P. A. (Eds.) (2004). *The Cult of the Saints in Late Antiquity and the Early Middle Ages: Essays on the Contribution of Peter Brown.* Oxford.
12. Zekiyan, B. L. (1982). Ełišē as Witness of the Ecclesiology of the Early Armenian Church. In N. G. Garsoïan, T. F. Mathews, & R. W. Thomson (Eds.) *East of Byzantium: Syria and Armenia in the Formative Period* (pp. 187-197). Harvard University.
13. Toumanoff, C. (1966). Armenia and Georgia. In J. M. Hussey (Ed.) *The Cambridge Medieval History, Volume IV* (pp. 593-637). Cambridge University Press.
14. Bonner, M. R. J. (2020). *The Last Empire of Iran.* Gorgias Press.

YEGHISHE'S

HISTORY

OF THE

VARTANANTS SAINTS

VOLUME I

ԴԱՒԹԻ ԵՐԻՑԻ ՄԱՄԻԿՈՆԻ ՀԱՅՑԵԱԼ

Զքանն վասն որոյ պատուիրեցեր՝ արարի, ո՛վ քաջ. վասն Հայոց պատերազմին հրամայեցեր, յորում բազումք առաքինացան քան զսակաւս:

Ահա նշանագրեցի յայսմ եւթն յեղանակիս.

Առաջին՝ զԺամանակն:

Երկրորդ՝ զԻրացն պատահումն յիշխանէն արեւելից:

Երրորդ՝ զՄիաբանութիւն ուխտին եկեղեցւոյ:

Չորրորդ՝ զԵրկպառակութիւն ոմանց բաժանելոց ի նմին ուխտէ:

Հինգերորդ՝ զՑարձակումն արեւելեայց:

Վեցերորդ՝ զԸնդդիմանալն Հայոց պատերազմաւ:

Եւթներորդ՝ զՑերկարումն իրացն խռովութեան:

Յայսմ յեւթն գլուխս կարգագրեալ եւ եդեալ ծայրալիր պատարմամբ զսկիզբն եւ զմիջոցն եւ զկատարումն, զի հանապազորդ ընթեռնուցուս, լսելով զառաքինեացն զքաջութիւն, եւ զյետս կացելոցն զվատթարութիւն. ոչ յանձին կարաւտութիւն երկրաւոր առատ գիտութեան լրման, այլ այցելութիւն երկնաւոր տնտեսութեան, որ մատակարարէ յառաջգիտութեամբ զհատուցմունս երկոցունց կողմանցն, որ երեւելեաւքն զաներեւոյթն գուշակէ:

UPON THE REQUEST OF THE PRIEST DAVID MAMIKON

I have composed this work that you have ordered, Your Excellency, about the Armenian war, in which our majority merited virtue.

I delineated this in these here seven chapters:

First, the period.

Second, what transpired because of the ruler of the East.

Third, on the brotherhood of the Church's faithful.

Fourth, on the dissension of some [of our compatriots] and their division from this brotherhood.

Fifth, on the attack of the Easterners.

Sixth, on the resistance of the Armenians in battle.

Seventh, on the prolongation of the troubles.

In these seven chapters, I have written an account, in full detail, of the beginning, middle, and end [of the war], that you may read it as a continuous narrative and hear of the valiance of the virtuous ones and the cowardice of the recreants—not for your want of fulfilling your worldly knowledge, which you hold in abundance, but for the visitation of heavenly providence which compensates us by its prescience, so that through the visible, the invisible is foretold.

Այլ դու, ո՛վ մեծդ ի գիտութեանն Աստուծոյ, առ ի՞նչ արդեւք հրամայեսցես, քան եթէ հրամայիցիս լաւագունացն: Որպէս երեւի ինձ եւ քեզ եւ այնոցիկ, որ դեգերեցին յիմաստասիրութեան, երկնաւոր սիրոյ է նշանակս այս եւ ոչ երկրաւոր փառասիրութեան. որպէս եւ ասացին իսկ ոմանք ի քաջ պատմագրացն. «Զուգութիւն է մայր բարեաց եւ անզուգութիւն ծնող չարեաց»:

Որպէս եւ մեր իսկ հայեցեալ ի սուրբ սէր քոյոյ հրամանիդ՝ ոչ ինչ դանդաղեալ վեհերեցաք հայեցեալ ի մեր տգիտութիւնս: Քանզի բազում ինչ է սրբութիւն՝ սատար լինել անաւսրութեան, որպէս աղաւթք գիտութեան, եւ սէր սուրբ՝ միաբան աւգտից:

Զոր եւ մեր ընդ հրամանին քում ընկալեալ՝ յաւժարութեամբ ձեռնարկեցաք զայս ինչ, որ է մխիթարութիւն սիրելեաց եւ յոյս յուսացելոց, քաջալերութիւն քաջաց, կամակարութեամբ յարձակեալ ի վերայ մահուան, յառաջոյ տեսանելով զզաւրագլուխն յաղթութեան, որ եւ ոչ ումեք ոտընհար լիցի թշնամութեամբ, այլ ամենեցուն ուսուցանէ զիւր անպարտելի զաւրութիւնն: Եւ ահա ո՛ ոք կամեսցի՝ ընդունի իբրեւ զնահատակ առաքինի: Եւ քանզի բազմադիմի է նահատակութեանդ անուն, եւ նա բազմադիմի շընորհիս բաշխէ ամենեցուն. զոր եւ մեծ իսկ քան զամենայն՝ սէր սուրբ յաննենգ մտաց գիտեմք:

But you, O great theologist, why would you command [me to compose this] when you could have commanded those who are better? As it appears to me, you, and those who persist in their love of wisdom, this is a sign of heavenly love and not a love of worldly glory. For as some of the erudite historians have said: "Parity is the mother of good; disparity, the parent of evil."

Upon seeing the holy love of your command, we neither tarried nor flinched, despite being aware of our ignorance, for holiness is a great support to meagerness, as prayer to understanding and holy love to the common good.

So when we received your command, we readily undertook this task as a consolation to our loved ones, as an aspiration for the hopeful [in Christ], and as encouragement to the brave, that they willingly attack death itself, seeing before them the victorious General who gloats over no one belligerently, but rather imparts His unconquerable power to all. For behold, whosoever wills, He accepts as a virtuous *nahatak*. And as the term nahatak has manifold meanings,[1] so too did He distribute His manifold grace to all, the greatest [aspect] of which we hold to be the holy love of a sincere mind.

1 *Nahatak* can refer to a martyr, warrior and/or hero.

DEDICATION

Այս պարզութիւն զվերնոյն բերէ զնմանութիւն. զոր եւ մեր ի քեզ տեսեալ, մոռացաք զմեր բնութիւնս: Եւ ահա վերաբերիմք ընդ քեզ ճախրելով, եւ իբրեւ բարձրաթռիչս եղեալ՝ զամենայն վնասակար մրրկածին աւդովք անցանիցեմք, եւ փոքր ի շատէ ծծելով յանապական վերին աւդոցն՝ առնուցումք զգիտութիւն ի փրկութիւն անձանց եւ ի փառս ամենայաղթ եկեղեցւոյ: Ուստի եւ բազում սուրբ պաշտաւնեայքն զուարթութեամբ կատարեցեն զսպաս վիճակին իւրեանց, ի փառս Հաւրն բոլորեցուն. ուր ընդ նմին սուրբ Երրորդութիւնն ցնծացեալ բերկրիցի յանտրտմական յիւրում էութեանն:

Արդ որովհետեւ ընկալաք զհրաման պատուիրանի յաննախանձ քոյոց բարուց բնութեանդ, սկսցուք ուստի արժան է սկսանել. թէպէտ եւ ոչ յաւժարիցեմք զթշուառութիւն ազգիս մերոյ ողբալ: Ահա ոչ ըստ կամաց արտաւսրալիր ողբովք ճառագրեմք զբազում հարուածս՝ յորում պատահեցաք եւ մեք իսկ ականատես լինելով:

This sincerity is in the likeness of heaven, and we, having seen it in you, have renounced our own nature. Now then we take flight and soar with you, and flying high we shall pass over all the dangerous tempests, and absorbing part of the pure air from above we shall obtain knowledge for the sake of our salvation and the glory of the all-conquering Church. Thus, let the many holy ministers cheefully hold service for the glory of the Father of all, where the Holy Trinity shall rejoice in its imperturbable essence.

Now as we have received this command from you, who are unenvious, let us begin where it is fit to do so. Yet, though we are not disposed to lament the calamity that befell our nation, it is not willingly that we relate with tearful laments the many blows we received and that we ourselves witnessed.

Ա

ԺԱՄԱՆԱԿՆ

Քանզի ի բառնալ ազգին Արշակունեաց, տիրեցին աշխարհիս Հայոց ազգն Սասանայ պարսկի, որ վարէր զիւր իշխանութիւնն աւրինաւք մոգուց. եւ բազում անգամ մարտնչէր ընդ այնոսիկ՝ որ ոչ ընդ նովին աւրինաւք մտանէին, սկիզբն արարեալ յամացն Արշակայ արքայի որդւոյն Տիրանայ, եւ կռուէր մինչեւ յամն վեցերորդ Արտաշիսի արքայի Հայոց, որդւոյն Վռամշապհոյ: Եւ իբրեւ զնա եւս մերժեաց ի թագաւորութենէն, ի նախարարսն Հայոց անկանէր թագաւորութիւնն. զի թէպէտ եւ զանձն յարքունիս Պարսկաց երթայր, սակայն այրուձին Հայոց բովանդակ ի ձեռն նախարացն առաջնորդէր ի պատերազմի: Վասն որոյ եւ աստուածպաշտութիւնն բարձրագլուխ կամակարութեամբ երեւելի լինէր յաշխարհին Հայոց, ի սկզբան տէրութեանն Շապհոյ արքայից արքայի մինչեւ յամն երկրորդ Յազկերտի արքայից արքայի՝ որդւոյ Վռամայ, զոր եգիտ սատանայ իւր գործակից, եւ զամենայն մթերեալ թոյնսն թափեաց ի բաց, եւ ելից զնա իբրեւ զպատկանդարան դեղեալ նետիւք: Եւ սկսաւ եղջեւր ածել անաւրէնութեամբ, գոռոզանայր, եւ գոռալով հողմն հանէր ընդ չորս կողմանս երկրի, եւ թշնամի եւ հակառակորդ երեւեցուցանէր իւր զհաւատացեալքս ի Քրիստոս, եւ նեղեալ տագնապէր անխաղաղասէր կենաւք:

I

THE PERIOD

After the fall of the Arsacid dynasty, the Sasanians of Persia ruled Armenia. They governed according to the customs of the magi, often oppressing those who did not follow their example,[2] starting with Arshak,[3] son of Tiran,[4] all the way to the sixth year of the reign of king Artashes,[5] son of Vramshapuh.[6] When [Artashes] was overthrown, his kingdom fell to the Armenian *nakharar*s, for although the tribute still went to the Persian royal, the cavalry was nonetheless fully under the control of the nakharars, who led them to war. Thus did Armenia hold its head high in piety from the accession of the king of kings, Shapur,[7] until the second year of the reign of the king of kings, Yazdegerd[8] (son of Bahram)[9] who was revealed to be an accomplice of Satan and who spat forth his venom like poisoned arrows from a quiver. Then like a brute he began to charge wickedly with his horns—puffed up with pride, bellowing, and kicking up dust over the whole face of the land—and made the faithful of Christ out to be his enemies and antagonists, and afflicted and terrorized them relentlessly.

---

2 *i.e.,* Zoroastrianism.
3 *Arshak II* (350-367).
4 *Tiran* (338-350).
5 *Artashes IV* (422-428).
6 *Vramshapuh* (389-417).
7 *Shapur II* (309-379).
8 *Yazdegerd II* (438-457).
9 *Bahram V* (420-438).

CHAPTER I

Քանզի յոյժ սիրելի էր նմա խռովութիւն եւ արիւնհեղութիւն, վասն այնորիկ յանձն իր տարաբերէր, եթէ յո՞ թափեցից զդառնութիւն թիւնաւոր, կամ ո՞ւր բացատրեցից զբազմութիւն նետիցն: Եւ առ յոյժ յիմարութեան իբրեւ զգազան կատաղի յարձակեցաւ ի վերայ աշխարհին Յունաց, եհար մինչ ի քաղաքն Մծբին, եւ բազում գաւառս Հոռոմոց աւերեաց ասպատակաւ, եւ զամենայն եկեղեցիս հրձիգ արար. կոտեաց զաւար եւ զգերի, եւ ահաբեկ արար զամենայն զաւրս աշխարհին:

Իսկ երանելին Թէոդոս կայսր, քանզի էր խաղաղասէր ի Քրիստոս, ոչ կամեցաւ ընդ առաջ նորա ելանել պատերազմաւ. այլ այր մի Անատոլ անուն, որ էր նորա սպարապետ արեւելից, առաքեաց առ նա բազում գանձիւք: Եւ արք պարսիկք, որք փախուցեալ էին վասն քրիստոնէութեան եւ էին ի քաղաքի կայսեր, կալաւ եւ ետ ի ձեռս նորա: Եւ զամենայն զոր ինչ ասաց ի ժամանակին՝ կատարեաց ըստ կամաց նորա, եւ արգել զնա ի բազում բարկութենէն, եւ դարձաւ անդրէն ի քաղաքն իւր Տիզբոն:

Եւ իբրեւ ետես անաւրէն իշխանն, եթէ յաջողեցաւ չարութիւն նորա, սկսաւ այլ եւս խորհուրդ յաւելուլ, որպէս ոք զի ի հուր բորբոքեալ յաւելու բազում նիւթս փայտից: Քանզի ուստի սակաւ մի կասկածոտն էր, անտի աներկիւղ հաստատեցաւ. վասն այնորիկ դրդուեցոյց զբազումս ի սուրբ ուխտէն քրիստոնէից, էր՝ զոր բանիւք սպառնալեաւք, էր՝ զոր կապանաւք եւ տանջանաւք, էր՝ զոր չարաչար մահուամբ վախճանէր:

Disorder and bloodshed were pleasing to him; therefore, he dithered over whom to spill his bitter poison on and where to shoot the multitude of his arrows. With great stupidity, he attacked the Greeks like a violent brute, pressed on as far as the city of Nisibis, despoiled many Roman districts, and set fire to all the churches. He carried away loot and prisoners and instilled terror among all the troops of the land.

Now the venerable Emperor Theodosius,[10] being peace-loving in Christ, would not give battle to the enemy; instead, he sent a man by the name of Anatolius, who was his general of the East, to meet Yazdegerd with many riches. [Anatolius] seized the Persian men who had fled because of Christianity and who were in the royal city, and delivered them into [Yazdegerd's] hands. [Anatolius] agreed to all of Yazdegerd's demands, appeased his great wrath, and returned to his city, Ctesiphon.

When the lawless ruler saw that his wickedness succeeded, he began to conspire more, as one adds fuel to fire. For not being prone to caution, he grew entrenched in fearlessness, on account of which he proceeded to stir everyone away from the holy brotherhood of the Christian faithful—some with mere threats, others with shackles and torments, and yet others with torturous deaths.

10 Theodosius II, 408-450.

CHAPTER I

Յափշտակութիւն առնէր ընչից եւ արարոց, եւ մեծաւ անարգանաւք տանջէր զամենեսեան: Եւ իբրեւ ետես՝ եթէ վայրատեալ ցրուեցան ի բազում կողմանս, ի խորհուրդ կըշէր զպաշտաւնեայս ձախակողմանն, որք կապեալ էին ի կըռապաշտութեանն անլուծանելի հանգուցիւք, վառեալք եւ ջեռեալք իբրեւ զհնոց առ այրել զուխտ սուրբ եկեղեցւոյ:

Քանզի էին իսկ այնպիսիքն բնակեալ ի կեանս իւրեանց իբրեւ ի թանձրամած խաւարի, եւ ոգիքն արգելեալք ի մարմնի իբրեւ զկենդանի ի գերեզմանի, յորս ամենեւին չծագէ նշոյլ սուրբ լուսոյն Քրիստոսի: Նա եւ արջք աւրհասականք ընդ վախճանել շնչոցն հզաւրագոյնք կռուին. յորոց եւ իմաստունքն տեղի տուեալ փախչին ի նոցանէ: Այսպիսի իմն եկեալ հասեալ է վախճան տէրութեանն. եթէ հարկանին՝ չզգան, եւ եթէ հարկանեն՝ չիմանան, եւ իբրեւ ոչ գտանի արտաքին թշնամի, ընդ անձինս իւրեանց մարտ եղեալ կռուին: Ի դէպ իսկ ելանէ բան մարգարէին ի վերայ նոցա, Այր, ասէ, առ քաղցի իւրում շրջեսցի եւ կերիցէ զկէս անձին իւրոյ: Սմին նման եւ Տէրն ինքնին ասէ. Ամենայն տուն եւ թագաւորութիւն՝ որ յանձն իւր բաժանի, ոչ կարէ կալ հաստատուն:

He seized their properties and possessions and tormented everyone with the grossest injustices. And when he saw that they had scattered to many lands, he held a council with his left-hand[11] ministers who were indissolubly bound to idolatry, inflamed like a furnace against the faithful of the holy church.

For people such as these live their lives as though plunged in darkness with their souls trapped in their bodies as though they were buried alive in tombs upon which not so much as a ray of the holy light of Christ shines. And just as bears put up the greatest fight when faced with death and wise men give way and flee from them, so too do the end of empires come about: When they are struck, they do not feel it; when they strike others, they do not perceive it; and when they fail to find an outside enemy, they fight amongst themselves. The following words of the prophet pertain to them: "Man, from hunger, devours half of himself."[12] Likewise, the Lord Himself says: "Every house and kingdom that is divided against itself cannot stand."[13]

---

11 *left hand:* alternatively, sinister.

12 Isaiah 9:20.

13 Mark 3:24-25.

CHAPTER I

Արդ զի՞ կոծիս, զի՞ մրցիս, զի՞ այրիս, զի՞ բորբոքիս, զի՞ չշիջանիս. զի՞ կոչես ի խորհուրդ զայնոսիկ, որոց զոգիսն ձեր ի ձէնջ քաղեալ՝ հանեալ է զանապականդ յապականութիւն, եւ զապականելի մարմինդ գէշաքարշ աարեալ իբրեւ զազիր մեռելոտի ի բաց ընկեցեալ: Ապաքէն զայդ կամիս, զի ծածկեսցի խորհուրդ ամբարշտութեանդ. տեսչիր յորժամ յայտնեսցի, ապա գիտասցես զելս կատարածի դորա:

Ասեն մոգքն. Արքայ քաջ, աստուածքն ետուն քեզ զտէրութիւնդ եւ զյաղթութիւն. եւ ոչ ինչ կարաւտ են նոքա մարմնաւոր մեծութեան, բայց եթէ ի մի աւրէնս դարձուցանես զամենայն ազգս եւ ազինս, որ են ի տէրութեան քում. յայնժամ եւ աշխարհն Յունաց հնազանդեալ մտցէ ընդ աւրինաւք քովք: Արդ զմի բան զմեր վաղվաղակի կատարեա դու, արքայ. զաւր գումարեա եւ գունդ կազմեա. խաղա գնա դու յերկիրն Քուշանաց. եւ զամենայն ազգս հաւաքեա եւ անցո ընտ Պահ դուռն ի ներքս. եւ դու անդէն արա քեզ բընակութիւն: Յորժամ արգելուս եւ փակես զամենեսեան ի հեռաւոր աւտարութեան, կատարին խորհուրդք կամաց քոց. եւ որպէս երեւիս մեզ ի դենիս մերում, տիրես դու եւ երկրին Քուշանաց, եւ Յոյնք իսկ ոչ ելանեն ընդ քո իշխանութիւնդ: Բայց միայն զաղանդ քրիստոնէից բարձ ի միջոյ:

Հաճոյ թուեցաւ խորհուրդն թագաւորին եւ մեծամեծացն, որ էին ի նմին բանի. հրովարտակս գրէր, պնդադեսպանս արձակէր յամենայն տեղիս տէրութեան իւրոյ:

Now then, what are you lamenting for? What are you fighting for? Why are you so provoked? Why don't you let up? Why do you keep conferring with those who seize your souls, treat the incorruptible as corruptible and your corruptible body as though it were a repulsive corpse? What you really wish for is to shut up your ungodly thoughts! Then keep an eye out for them, and you shall know when they arise.

The magi said: "Valiant king, the gods have given you lordship and victory: they require no mortal honors; but look to it that all the peoples and nations of your kingdom be brought under one rule—then you will also subject the land of the Greeks to your rule. Now do immediately as we say, king; gather an army, equip your troops and advance against the land of the Kushans. Assemble all the nations, lead them through *Pah Durn*[14] and set up camp there. When you hold them all fast in a distant foreign land, the object of your wishes will be attained. If you dignify our religion, then you will rule over the land of the Kushans and not even the Greeks will make inroads into your territory. But only do away with the Christian sect!"

The advice was pleasing to the king and his grandees. He wrote an edict and dispatched messengers throughout his kingdom.

---

14 *Pah Durn:* "The Gate of the Guard".

CHAPTER I

Եւ այս է պատճէն հրովարտակին.

Առ ամենայն ազգս տէրութեան իմոյ՝ արեաց եւ անարեաց, բազմացի ի ձեզ ողջոյն մարդասիրութեան մերոյ. դուք ողջ լերուք, եւ մեք մեզէն ողջ եմք դիցն աւգնականութեամբ: Առանց զձեզ ինչ աշխատ առնելոյ խաղացաք գնացաք յերկիրն Յունաց, եւ առանց գործոյ պատերազմի սիրով մարդասիրութեամբ նուաճեցաք զամենայն երկիրն մեզ ի ծառայութիւն: Դուք զքարի զմտաւ ածէք, եւ անսպառ լերուք յուրախութեան. բայց զայս բան կատարեցէք վաղվաղակի, զոր ասեմ: Մեք ի մտի եդաք անվրէպ խորհրդովք խաղալ գնալ յաշխարհն արեւելից, աստուածոցն աւգնականութեամբ դարձուցանել ի մեզ զտէրութիւնն Քուշանաց. դուք իբրեւ զհրովարտակս զայս տեսանէք, անխափան վաղվաղակի այրուձի գումարեցէք առաջոյ քան զիս, յանդիման լինիջիք ինձ յԱպար աշխարհին:

Ըստ այսմ պատճենի հրովարտակ եհաս յաշխարհն Հայոց, ի Վրաց եւ յԱղուանից, եւ ի Լփնաց, ի Ծաւդէից եւ ի Կորդուաց, յԱղձնեաց եւ բազում այլ տեղեաց հեռաւորաց, որոց ոչ էին աւրէնք երթալ զայն ճանապարհ յառաջ ժամանակաւ: Գունդ կազմէր ի Հայոց Մեծաց զազատ եւ զազատորդի, եւ յարքունի տանէ զոստանիկ մարդիկ. բստ նըմին աւրինակի ի Վրաց եւ յԱղուանից եւ յաշխարհէն Լըփնաց, եւ որ այլ եւս ի կողմանց կողմանց հարաւոյ մերձ ի սահմանս Տաճկաստանի եւ ի Հոռոմց աշխարհն եւ ի Կորդուաց եւ ի Դասն եւ ի Ծաւդէ եւ յԱրզնարզին, որք էին մեներքեան հաւատացեալք եւ մկրտեալք ի մի կաթողիկէ եւ առաքելական եկեղեցի:

This is a copy of the edict:

> *To all the peoples of my kingdom, Aryans and non-Aryans,*[15] *many greetings to you all from our benevolent rule. May it be well with you as it is well with us with the help of the gods. Without troubling you in the slightest, we advanced to the land of the Greeks and without so much as making war we benevolently submitted the whole country in vassalage to us. Be of good cheer and rejoice unboundedly, but immediately fulfill the following: We have formed an unfailing resolution to march on the land of the East, and, with the help of the gods, to return the Kushans back to our rule. Regard this as a decree: you will immediately, and without delay, assemble your cavalry before me and accompany me to the land of Apar.*[16]

Now this edict reached Armenia, Georgia and Aghuank, as well as Lpink, Tsodik, Korduk, Aghtsnik and many other lands which in former times were not obliged to join these expeditions. An army of *azat*s and their sons was formed in Greater Armenia, including nobles from the royal house and those from Iberia, Aghuank, Lpink, from the lands to the south as far as the border of Tachkastan, as well as from the lands of the Romans and the Korduk, and from Dasn, Tsode and Arznarziv, who were all faithful and had been baptized in the One Catholic and Apostolic Church.

15 *Aryans and non-Aryans:* Iranians and non-Iranians.

16 *Apar:* Khorasan.

Եւ անմեղութեամբ ոչ գիտացեալ զերկդիմի միտս թագաւորին՝ խաղացին գնացին յիւրաքանչիւր աշխարհաց լրջմտութեամբ եւ տիրասէր խորհրդովք, կատարել զպաս զինուորութեան աներկբայ հաւատովք: Բարձին եւս ընդ իւրեանս զաստուածային զսուրբ կտակարանսն բազում պաշտաւնէիւք եւ քահանայիւք: Բայց հրաման տուեալ աշխարհի՝ ոչ իբրեւ յակնկալութիւն կենաց, այլ իբրեւ ի վրճարումն վախճանի, յանձն առնելով միմեանց զոգիս եւ զմարմինս: Զի թէպէտ եւ խորհուրդ թագաւորին չէր յայտնեալ նոցա, սակայն կարծիք ի մտի էին ամենեցուն. մանաւանդ իբրեւ բեկեալ տեսանէին զզաւրութիւնն Յունաց առաջի նորա, յոյժ հարեալ խոցեցան ի խորհուրդս իւրեանց:

Բայց քանզի պատուիրանապահք էին սուրբ կտակարանացն Աստուծոյ, հանապազ յիշէին զպատուիրեալսն ի Պաւղոսէ, եթէ Ծառայք, հպատակ լերուք տերանց ձերոց մարմնաւորաց. մի՛ սուտակաապաք եւ առաչս աչառելով. այլ սրտի մտաւք ծառայեցէք իբրեւ Աստուծոյ եւ մի՛ իբրեւ մարդկան. քանզի ի Տեառնէ է հատուցումն արդար վաստակոց ձերոց:

Եւ այսու ամենայնիւ բարեմտութեամբ յուղարկեալք յաշխարհէ եւ յանձն եղեալք սուրբ Հոգւոյն, յանդիման լինէին՝ փութով կատարեալ զհրամանն, եւ զամենայն արարեալ ըստ կամաց նորա: Յոյժ ուրախ լինէր թագաւորն, իբր այն եթէ կատարեցան կամք կարծեաց նորա. եւ ահա առնէր ընդ նոսա զայն ինչ, զոր պաշտաւնեայքն ամբարշտութեան նորա խրատեցին:

Innocently, they had not suspected the two-faced design of the king: they advanced, each from his land, cheerfully, ready to serve their master and to carry out their soldierly service with undivided faith. There were also many officials and priests with them, along with the Holy Testaments of God. Yet the edict was not presented to the country in the expectation of life, but as a debt to death of both soul and body. For although the king had not conveyed his intent to them, the possibility was now in everyone's mind. They were greatly troubled in their thoughts, especially because they had seen how the strength of the Greeks was shattered before him.

But they remained obedient to the Holy Testaments of God and constantly recalled the commandments of Paul: "Be obedient servants to your earthly masters; be not opposed to them, but show them homage; serve them in love, as though you were serving God and not man: for the Lord shall reward you for all your pains."[17]

Nonetheless, they left their country in good will, committed themselves to the Holy Spirit, and were ready to comply at once with [the king's] orders, and to carry out all things according to his wishes. The king rejoiced as though they had fulfilled his wishes, but then proceeded to do with them as he had been advised by his impious ministers.

---

17 Ephesians 6:5-9.

CHAPTER I

Ապա իբրեւ ետես թագաւորն զամենայն կազմութիւն եւ զբազմութիւն գնդին բարբարոսաց, որք սրտի մտաւք եկեալ էին ի վաստակ արքունի, առաւելապէս եւս ուրախ լինէր առաջի մեծամեծացն եւ ամենայն բազմութեան զաւրաց իւրոց: Ի վերին երեսս թաքուցանէր զկամս մտաց իւրոց, եւ ակամայ առատապէս պարգեւէր զնոսա: Խաղաց գնաց միանգամայն ի վերայ տէրութեան Հոնաց աշխարհին, զոր Քուշանս անուանեն. եւ զերկեամ մի կռուեալ՝ ոչ ինչ կարաց ազդել նոցա: Ապա արձակեաց զմարզիկսն յիւրաքանչիւր տեղիս, եւ զայլս փոխանակ նոցա առ իւր կոչեաց նովին պատրաստութեամբ: Եւ այսպէս ամ յամէ սովորութիւն կարգեաց, եւ իւր անդէն քաղաք բնակութեան շինեաց, սկսեալ ի չորրորդ ամէ տէրութեանն իւրոյ մինչեւ յամն մետասաներորդ թագաւորութեանն:

Եւ իբրեւ ետես, եթէ հաստատուն կացին Հոռոմք յուխտին իւրեանց, զոր եդին ընդ նմա, եւ դադարեցին Խայլնդուրք ելանել ընդ պահակն Ճորայ, եւ յամենայն կողմանց խաղաղութեամբ բնակեաց աշխարհ նորա, եւ ի նեղ եւս էարկ զթագաւորն Հոնաց, քանզի աւերեաց զբազում գաւառս նորա եւ յաջողեցաւ տէրութիւն նորա, աւետաւորս առաքեաց ընդ ամենայն ատրուշանս աշխարհին իւրոյ. ցլուք սպիտակաւք եւ գիսաւոր նոխազաւք առատացոյց զզոհս կրակի, եւ խիտ առ խիտ թանձրացոյց անդուլութեամբ զպաշտաւն պղծութեան իւրոյ. պսակաւք եւ պատուովք մեծարեաց զբազումս ի մոգաց եւ զբազմագոյնս ի մոգպետաց: Ետ եւս հրաման յափշտակել զամենայն ինչս քրիստոնէից եւ զստացուածս, որք էին ի մէջ Պարսկաց աշխարհին:

When the king saw the whole assembly of barbarian troops who had cheerfully hastened to serve him, he displayed great satisfaction once more before the grandees and his whole army. Concealing his intentions, he reluctantly showered gifts upon them. He advanced at once against the kingdom of the Huns, who are called Kushans; but despite two years of war, he could not do a thing against them. Then he released the troops, each to his own place, and summoned others in their place for a new round of preparations. Thus he established this custom year after year, and built himself a city there, which he inhabited from the fourth year of his reign until the eleventh.

When the king saw that the Romans had remained true to their oath to him, that the *Khaylndurk*[18] had stopped crossing the gate of Chor, that peace reigned throughout all his dominions and that the king of the Huns was left in even greater straits (for he had devastated many [Hunnic] districts and succeeded over his dominion), he sent joyful tidings to all the fire-temples in his land, had white bulls and long-haired goats brought and sacrificed abundantly to the fire, and unceasingly multiplied his impure Service; he honored the magi (and much more, the mogbeds) with crowns and other marks of distinction. He then intercepted a command addressed to the Christians who were in the land of the Persians.

18 *Khaylndurk:* the royal army of the Caucasian Huns.

CHAPTER I

Եւ այսպէս հպարտացաւ բարձրացաւ ի միտս իւր, ի վեր քան զմարդկային բնութիւն ընդվզեալ ապարթանէր ոչ միայն յիրս մարմնական պատերազմացն, այլ մեծ ոմն զինքն կարծէր քան զբնութիւն հայրենի կարգին. վասն այնորիկ կեղծաւորութեամբ թագուցանէր զինքն ըստ կարծեացն, եւ որպէս երեւէր իմաստնոցն, յանմահից իմն կարգի դնէր զինքն: Եւ յոյժ էր ցասուցեալ ընդ անունն Քրիստոսի, յորժամ լսէր՝ թէ տանջեցաւ, խաչեցաւ, մեռաւ եւ թաղեցաւ:

Եւ իբրեւ այսպէս աւր ըստ աւրէ ի սոյն միտս ցնորեալ դանդաչէր, մի ոմն մանկագոյն ի նախարարացն Հայոց ընդդէմ բանս եդ եւ ասէ. «Արքայ քաջ, դու ուստի՞ գիտես զայդպիսի բանս խաւսել զՏեառնէ»: Ետ պատասխանի թագաւորն եւ ասէ. «Իմ իսկ առաջի ընթերցան զգիրս մոլորութեան ձերոյ»: Ետ պատասխանի անդրէն պատանեակն եւ ասէ. «Ընդէ՞ր, արքայ, ցայդ վայր միայն ետուր ընթեռնուլ. այլ յառաջ եւս մատո զկարդացումն, եւ լսես անդ զյարութիւնն, զյայտնութիւնն առ բազումս, զվերացումն յերկինս, զնստելն ընդ աջմէ Հաւր, զխոստումն երկրորդ գալստեանն՝ զհրաշակերտ յարութիւնն առնելով բոլորեցունց. զհամառաւտ հատուցմունսն արդար դատաստանին»: Իբրեւ լուաւ զայս թագաւորն, ի խոր խոցեալ՝ վեր ի վերոյ ծիծաղեցաւ եւ ասէ. «Այդ ամենայն խաբէութիւն է»: Ետ պատասխանի զինուորն Քրիստոսի եւ ասէ. «Եթէ հաւատարիմ են քեզ մարմնաւոր չարչարանքն նորա, հաւատարմագոյն եւս լիցի քեզ երկրորդ ահաւոր գալուստն նորա»:

Thus he grew so high and mighty in his own estimation that he boastfully exalted himself even above human nature—not only in physical warfare, but even in holding himself above his own paternal rank. He duplicitously concealed his intention and fancying himself wise, placed himself in the rank of the immortals. He then uttered great reproaches against the name of Christ when he understood that the Lord had been tortured and crucified, and that He died and was buried.

As the king was boasting and raving like this day after day, one of the younger Armenian nakharars contradicted him and said: "Valiant king, how did you come to learn such words as you now utter against the Lord?" The king replied, "They have read your aberrant books before me." The youth replied, "Why, king, did you only read so far? Continue reading further and you will hear of His resurrection, His epiphany before many, His ascension to heaven, His seat at the right-hand of the Father, His promise of His Second Coming, and the miraculous resurrection of all; in a word, you will hear of the reward of the just Judgment." When the king heard this, he was deeply struck, and laughed and laughed, and said: "That is all deceit." The soldier of Christ replied and said: "If you find His bodily tortures believable, so too must you believe in His awesome Second Coming."

Եւ զայս լսելով թագաւորին՝ բորբոքեցաւ իբրեւ զհուր հնոցին ի Բաբիլոն, մինչ եւ իւրքն իսկ անդէն դեռ եւս իբրեւ զքաղդէացիսն այրեցեալ լինէին:

Յայնժամ զբոլոր բարկութիւն սրտմտութեանն եհեղ յայրն երանելի, որում անուն էր Գարեգին: Կապեալ ոտիւք եւ կապեալ ձեռաւք զերկեամ մի տուաւ ի չարչարանս, եւ հանեալ ի բաց զտէրութիւնն ի նմանէ՝ ընկալաւ զվճիռ մահու:

Having heard these words, the king blazed like the fire of the furnace in Babylon, inflaming those who were present, just as the Chaldeans had been.

Then the full measure of his rage poured angrily upon the blessed man, whose name was Karekin. Fettering his feet and binding his hands, he put him to torture for two years, deprived him of his rank, and had him killed.

Բ

ԻՐԱՑՆ ՊԱՏԱՀՈՒՄՆ ՅԻՇԽԱՆԷՆ ԱՐԵՒԵԼԻՑ

Որոց ոգիքն թուլացեալ են յերկնաւոր առաքինութենէն՝ յոյժ ընդ ահիւ անկեալ է բնութիւն մարմնոյ. յամենայն հողմոյ շարժի, եւ յամենայն բանէ խռովի, եւ յամենայն իրաց դողայ. երազագէտ է այնպիսին ի կեանս իւրում, եւ յանգիւտ կորուստն յուղարկի ի մահուան իւրում: Որպէս եւ ասաց ոմն ի հնումն, մահ ոչ իմացեալ՝ մահ է, մահ իմացեալ՝ անմահութիւն է: Որ զմահ ոչ գիտէ, երկնչի ի մահուանէ. իսկ որ գիտէ զմահ, ոչ երկնչի ի նմանէ:

Եւ այս ամենայն չարիք մտանեն ի միտս մարդոյ յանուսումնութենէ: Կոյր զրկի ի ճառագայթից արեգական, եւ տգիտութիւն զրկի ի կատարեալ կենաց: Լաւ է կոյր աչաւք քան կոյր մտաւք: Որպէս մեծ է ոգի քան զմարմին՝ այսպէս մեծ է տեսաւորութիւն մտաց քան զմարմնոյ:

Եթէ ոք կարի առաւելեալ իցէ աշխարհական մեծութեամբ, եւ մտաւքն աղքատագոյն, այնպիսին ողորմելի է քան զբազումս. որպէս եւ տեսանեմք իսկ՝ ոչ միայն ի չափաւոր մարդիկ, այլ եւ յոր մեծն է քան զամենայն: Թագաւոր եթէ ոչ ունի զիմաստութիւն աթոռակից իւր, ոչ կարէ ի վիճակին իւրում վայելուչ գոլ: Իսկ եթէ առ մարմնաւորս այսպէս, ո՞րչափ եւս առաւել առհոգեւորն:

II

WHAT TRANSPIRED BECAUSE OF THE RULER OF THE EAST

Those whose souls are slack in heavenly virtue have had their corporeal natures fall into dread; shaken by every wind, perturbed by every word, made to tremble at every turn, such a person dreams throughout life and is sent to his irretrievable destruction at death. As someone of old said, "Death not understood is mortality; death understood is immortality." He who does not know death fears it, but he who knows death is not afraid of it.

All these evils enter people's minds through a lack of learning. As blindness deprives one from the light of the sun, so does ignorance deprive one from living a consummate life. But it is better to be blind of eyes than blind of mind, for just as the soul is greater than the body, so too is the vision of the mind greater than the body's.

If one can abound in worldly greatness, yet be of penurious mind, then he is more pitiable than most; we see the same not only among commoners, but also in the one who ranks above all: If a king does not rule with wisdom, then he cannot be favored in his rank. And if it is so in the physical realm, then it is much more so in the spiritual!

CHAPTER II

Բոլոր մարմնոյս հոգի է կենդանութիւն, իսկ մարմնոյ եւ հոգւոյ միտք են կառավար. եւ որպէս առ մի մարդ՝ այսպէս առ բոլոր աշխարհս: Թագաւոր ոչ զիւրն միայն տացէ պարտիս, այլ եւ որոց եղեւ պատճառք ի կորուստ:

Բայց մեք թէպէտ եւ ոչ ունիմք հրաման բամբասել զիշխանս, եւ ոչ գովողք կարեմք լինել այնմիկ՝ որ աստուածամարտն լինիցի: Այլ զանցսիրացն պատմեմ, որ ի նմանէ ընդ սուրբ եկեղեցիսն էանց, եւ ոչ դանդաղիմ. ոչ բամբասաւէր մտաւք, այլճշմարտութեամբ զելս իրացն ասելով ոչ լռեցից: Ոչ ի կարծ ընդոստուցեալ, եւ ոչ ի լուր զարթուցեալ. այլ ես ինքնին անձամբ անդէն ի տեղւոջն պատահեցի եւ տեսի եւ լուայ զձայն բարբառոյ յանդգնաբար խաւսելով. իբրեւ զհողմ սաստիկ՝ զի բախիցէ զծով մեծ, այնպէս շարժէր եւ տատանէր զամենայն բազմութիւն զաւրաց իւրոց: Եւ հանդէս առնէր ամենայն ուսմանց, եւ ընդաճէր զմոգութիւնն եւ զքաւդէութիւնն եւ զամենայն ուսմունս աշխարհին իւրոյ: Արկանէր ի ներքս եւ զքրիստոնէութիւն կեղծաւորութեամբ, եւ ասէր զայրացեալ մտաւք. «Հարցէք, քննեցէք, տեսէք. թող որ լաւն է՛ընտրեալ կալցուք»: Եւ փութայր որ ինչ ի մտին էր, զի վաղվաղակի կատարեսցէ:

Իսկ ի կողմանց կողմանց քրիստոնեայքն, որ ի զաւրուն էին, իմացան զհուրն որ ի ծածուկ վառեալ բորբոքէր, եւ կամէր հրդեհել զլերինս եւ զդաշտս առհասարակ: Ջեռան եւ նոքա անծախական հրովն, եւ սաստկապէս պատրաստեցան առ ի փորձութիւն զաղտնի մեքենայիցն:

The entire body is animated by the soul, and the body and the soul are driven by the mind: It is so for one man as it is for all the world. And a king is not only accountable for himself, but also for those whom he has been a cause of destruction.

But although we are not permitted to speak against the ruler, neither can we praise a man who would fight against God. Now let me recount what happened because of what he did against the holy church, and without delay: not with the intent of condemning him, but so as not to be silent from delivering the truth about what happened. Nor do I do this to stir suspicion or awaken rumors. For I myself happened to be there and saw and heard the sound of his impudent voice, and as the powerful wind stirs the great sea, so did he rouse and excite the multitude of his forces. He reviewed all their doctrines and propagated Magiansm, divination and all the doctrines of his land. He deceitfully brought up Christianity among these, and said with rage: "Probe, examine and observe these, and let us hold fast to the good," but then hurried to immediately carry out what he had in his mind.

Then the Christians who were in different parts of the army came to understand that there was a fire that had been burning in secret, and that it threatened to burn up everything from the mountains to the valleys. They, too, burned with an unquenchable fire, boldly preparing themselves for the trials of the king's secret machinations.

CHAPTER II

Սկսան այնուհետեւ բարձր բարբառով, սաղմոսիւք եւ երգովք հոգեւորաւք եւ մեծապայծառ վարդապետութեամբ յայտ յանդիման մեծի բանակին զպաշտաւնն ցուցանել. եւ աներկիւղ առանց զանգիտելոյ՝ ո՛ ոք եւ երթայր առ նոսա, ուսուցանէին կամակար: Եւ Տէր յաջողէր նոցա նշանաւք եւ արուեստիւք. քանզի բազում հիւանդք ընդունէին զբժշկութիւն ի հեթանոսական զաւրուէն:

Իսկ անաւրէն իշխանն իբրեւ գիտաց եթէ յայտնեցաւ խորամանկութիւն խորհրդոյն, եւ պատրաստեալ հուրն՝ մինչչեւ ուրուք ի նա փչեալ՝ վառումն նորայայտնի իմացաւ երկիւղածացն Աստուծոյ, սկսաւ ծածուկ նետիւք խոցոտել զմիտս իւրոյ չարութեանն. եւ անբժշկական վէրս յոգիս եւ ի մարմինս տեսանէր: Մերթ շանթէր գալարէր իբրեւ զաւձ թիւնաւոր, մերթ պարզէր գոչէր իբրեւ զառիւծ զայրացեալ. գելոյր, գլորէր, տապալէր երկդիմի մտաւք եւ զխորհուրդս կամացն կամէր կատարել: Քանզի ձեռն արկանել եւ ունել ոչ կարէր, վասն զի ոչ էին համագունդ ի միում վայրի առ նմա, սկսաւ այնուհետեւ յառաջ կոչել զկրսերս յաւագաց եւ զանարգս ի պատուականաց եւ զտգէտս ի գիտնոց եւ զանարիս ի քաջ արանց. եւ զի՞ մի մի թուիցեմ, այլ զամենայն զանարժանսն յառաջ մատուցանէր եւ զամենայն զարժանաւորսն յետս տանէր. մինչեւ զհայր եւ զորդի քակէր ի միմեանց:

They began thereafter to loudly sing psalms and other spiritual songs and performed brilliant teachings and acts of worship before the great army. They fearlessly and willingly taught anyone who came to them, and the Lord prospered them with signs and wonders, for many of those who were ill in the army of the heathens were healed.

When the lawless ruler saw that his cunning purpose had become known, and that the fire that he had prepared became known to those who fear God before anyone had even fanned the flames, he began to pierce his own evil mind with hidden arrows, thus inflicting incurable wounds to his soul and body. Bursting and coiling like a poisonous serpent, rising and roaring like a raging lion, he writhed, twisted and turned in his duplicitous mind and resolved to fulfill his schemes. But since he could not lay his hands on the Christians, for they were not all assembled together in the same place, he started calling forth youth to replace elders, the contemptible to replace the honorable, the ignorant to replace the knowledgeable and cowards to replace brave men. But why shall I go on enumerating these? For he promoted all those who were unworthy and relegated the worthy ones to the point that he even loosened fathers from sons.

CHAPTER II

Թէպէտ եւ ընդ ամենայն ազգս առնէր զանկարգութիւնս զայս, առաւել ընդ Հայոց աշխարհին մարտնչէր. քանզի տեսանէր զնոսա ջերմագոյնս յաստուածպաշտութեան, մանաւանդ որք էին յազգէ նախարարացն Հայոց, եւ անմեղութեամբ ունէին զսուրբ քարոզութիւն առաքելոցն եւ զմարգարէից: Պատրէր զոմանս ի նոցանէ ոսկւով եւ արծաթով, եւ զբազումս այլով եւս առատ պարգեւաւք. իսկ զոմանս ագարակաւք եւ մեծամեծ գեղաւք, զոմանս պատուովք եւ իշխանութեամբք մեծամեծաւք: Եւ այլ եւս սնոտի յոյս ոգւոց առաջին դնէր. եւ այսպէս հրապուրէր եւ յորդորէր համապազ. «Եթէ միայն, ասէ, զաւրէնս մոգութեան յանձին կալջիք, եւ զձեր մոլորութիւնդ սրտի մտաւք դարձուսջիք ի ճշմարտութիւն երեւելի մերոց դից աւրինացս, ի մեծութիւնս եւ յաւագութիւնս հասուցից հաւասար իմոյ սիրելի նախարարացս, եւ առաւել եւս զանցուցից»: Եւ այսպէս կեղծաւորութեամբ խոնարհեցուցանէր զինքն առ ամենեսեան, խաւսելով ընդ նոսա ի պատճառս սիրոյ, զի խոնարհամանկութեամբ որսալ մարթասցէ զնոսա ըստ առաջին խորհրդականացն խրատուց: Եւ զայս առնէր սկսեալ ի չորրորդ ամէն մինչեւ մետասաներորդ ամն իւրոյ տէրութեանն:

Although he caused disorder in every nation, he fought the Armenians more than all the rest, for he observed that they were the most zealous in the service of God—especially those who were from the families of the nakharars, and who blamelessly held to the holy sermons of the apostles and prophets. He won some of them over with gold and silver, and others with many presents; some with farms and large villages, and others with honors and great authority. Then he put other vain hopes before their souls, and thus continued to bribe and exhort them: "If only," he said, "you would conform yourselves to Magian customs, and turn from your errant ways to the worship of our prominent divinities, you would then stand equal to my own dear nobles in greatness and distinction, and I would exalt you still higher." Thus, he humbled himself deceitfully before everyone, speaking on the pretext of love to lure them with tricks, according to the initial counsel of his advisors. He did this from the fourth to the 11th year of his reign.

CHAPTER II

Եւ իբրեւ ետես եթէ ոչինչ յարգեցաւ ծածուկ հնարագիտութիւնն, այլ ընդդէմքն յոլովագոյն գործէին, քանզի տեսանէր զքրիստոնէութիւն, որ աւրքան զաւր յորդեալ տարածանէր ընդ ամենայն կողմանս հեռաւոր ճանապարհին ընդ որ ինքն անցանէր, սկսաւ հաշել եւ մաշել եւ հառաչելով յոգւոց հանել: Յայտնեաց ակամայ զծածուկ խորհուրդսն. եւ հրաման բարձր բարբառով եւ ասէ. «Ամենայն ազգ եւ լեզուք՝ որ են ընդ իմով իշխանութեամբ՝ դադարեսցեն յիւրաքանչիւր մոլոր աւրինաց, եւ միայնոյ եկեսցեն յերկրպագութիւն արեգական, զոհս մատուցանելով եւ աստուած անուանելով, եւ սպաս ունելով կրակի. եւ ի վերայ այսր ամենայնի եւ զմոգութեան աւրէնս կատարելով, զի մի՛ ինչ ամենեւին պակաս առնիցեն»:

Զայս ասելով քարոզ կարդայր ի մեծի կարաւանին, եւ պատուէր սաստիւ ի վերայ դնէր ամենեցուն. եւ դեսպանս ստիպաւ արձակէր յամենայն ազգս հեռաւորս, զդոյն պատուէր հրամանի առ ամենեսեան արկանէր:

Արդ ի սկզբան երկոտասաներորդ ամի թագաւորութեան իւրոյ գունդ կազմէր անհամար բազմութեամբ, յարձակեալ հասանէր յերկիրն Իտաղական: Զայս տեսեալ թագաւորին Քուշանաց՝ ոչ հանդուրժէր ելանել ընդ առաջ նորա պատերազմաւ. այլ խոյս տուեալ ի կողմանս ամուր անապատին, թագստեամբ ապրէր հանդերձ ամենայն զաւրաւքն իւրովք: Իսկ սաասպատակ արձակէր գաւառաց, տեղեաց, վայրաց. առնոյր զքազում բերդս եւ զքաղաքս, եւ կուտէր զգերին, զառ եւ զապուռ եւ զաւար, ածէր հասուցանէր յերկիր իւրոյ տէրութեանն:

However, when he observed that his cunning devices were not respected, and, on the contrary, that his opponents accomplished more because of this, so that Christianity grew stronger and spread itself through even the distant countries through which he had passed, he became sullen, and was consumed, and sighed and sighed. He unwittingly revealed his secret intention, commanding loudly: "All the nations and tongues throughout my dominions must abandon their errant customs and only worship the sun, offering sacrifices to it, calling it god and administering the fire cult; and on top of all this, they must fulfil all the other Magian ordinances, and nothing less."

Saying this, he addressed the great multitude of the caravan and gave strict commands to all. Then he quickly dispatched ambassadors to all the distant nations and delivered the same command to them all.

At the beginning of the 12th year of his reign he assembled an innumerably large army and entered the land of Itaghakan.[19] The king of the Kushans saw this but could not stand to go before them in battle, so he took flight toward the dense wilderness and thus escaped with his entire army. Then, [Yazdegerd II] sent troops into all the districts and regions [of the Kushans]: He seized many fortresses and cities, gathered captives, took spoils and plunder and bore them away to his dominion.

---

19 *Itaghakan:* possibly, Հեփթաղական (*Heptaghakan*), of the Hephthalites.

CHAPTER II

Եւ անդ այնուհետեւ յընդունայն եղեալ ի նոյն խոր-հուրդս՝ հաստատէր ի կարծիս մոլորութեան, ասելով ցպաշտաւնեայս ամբարշտութեանն. «Զի՞նչ հատուցուք մեք աստուածոցն փոխանակ այս մեծ ի յաղթութեանս, որ ոչ ոք կարաց ելանել ընդդէմ մեր պատերազմաւ»: Յայնմ ժամանակի առ հասարակ մոգք եւ քաւդեայք բարձին զձայնս իւրեանց միաբան եւ ասեն. «Աստուածքն որ ետուն քեզ զտէրութիւն եւ զյաղթութիւն ի վերայ թշնամեաց քոց, ոչ ինչ են կարաւտ խնդրել ի քէն յերեւելի պատուականացս, այլ զի բարձցես զամենայն ուսմունս մոլորութեան մարդ-կան, եւ ի մի դարձուցես աւրէնս զրադաշտական պատ-ուիրանին»:

Հաճոյ թուէր բանն առաջի թագաւորին եւ ամենայն մեծամեծացն, մանաւանդոր էին առաջակայք աւրինացն: Խորհուրդ ի մէջ առեալ յաղթէր խրատն: Անդէն ի ներքոյ Պահ դրանն արգելոյր զբազմութիւն այրուձիոյն Հայոց եւ զՎրաց եւ զԱղուանից, եւ զամենեցուն՝ որ էին հաւատաց-եալ ի սուրբ աւետարանն Քրիստոսի: Եւ հրաման սաս-տիւ դռնապանացն առնէին, եթէ որ յարեւելս առ մեզ գայ-ցէ՝ թողցեն, իսկ յարեւելից յարեւմուտս անանց լիցի ճա-նապարհ:

Եւ իբրեւ արգել եւ փակեաց զնոսա յամուր եւ յանել գառագիղն,—եւ յիրաւի ասացի ամուր եւ անել, քանզի չիք անդ տեղի փախստի եւ թաքստի, վասն զի շուրջանակի թշնամիք են բնակեալ,—յայնմ ժամանակի ձեռն արկանէրի նոսա, եւ մեծաւ չարչարանաւք եւ պէսպէս տանջանաւք վատթարէր զբազումս ի նոցանէ, եւ ստիպէր ուրանալ զճըշ-մարիտն աստուած, եւ խոստովանել զերեւելի տարերս:

Thereafter, persisting in the same vain intention, he held firm to his stray thoughts, telling his impious ministers: "What shall we give the gods in exchange for this great triumph, such that no one was able to oppose us in battle?" At this time the magi and astrologers raised their voices in unison and said: "The gods, who have given you empire and victory over your enemies, require no other signs of homage from you than that you should banish all errant doctrines of man, and turn [their] customs to the Zoroastrian command."

This speech found favor before the king and all the grandees, and especially those of the highest religious rank. They took counsel and favored that advice. Then, within the Gate of the Guard he enclosed the host of Armenian, Georgian and Aghuanian cavalry, and all others who were believers in the Holy Gospel of Christ. The gatekeepers received strict orders to let everyone who was coming eastward to pass, but to block the road for those going from east to west.

When they were thus hemmed into that strong and inescapable prison—and truly strong and inescapable, for there was nowhere to run or hide, as the enemy dwelt all around—that's when he threw his hands on them and inflicted great pains and various tortures, that they might be forced to deny the true God and confess the visible elements.

Իսկ զաւրականքն առհասարակ գեղեցիկ խորհրդով, քաջապէս զաւրութեամբ միաբան աղաղակէին եւ ասէին. «Վկայ են մեզ երկինք եւ երկիր, որ ոչ երբէք հեղ գացեալ եմք յարքունի վաստակս, եւ ոչ խառնեալ վատութիւն ընդ արութիւն քաջութեան. ի զուր եւ անողորմ են հարուածքս ի վերայ մեր»:

Եւ բազմանայր գոչումն աղաղակի նոցա, մինչեւ ինքնին թագաւորն ականատես լինէր իրացն յանդիմանութեան, եւ անդէն վաղվաղակի երդմամբ հաստատէր եւ ասէր. «Ոչ թողացուցից ձեզ, մինչեւ կատարեսջիք զամենայն կամս հրամանաց իմոց:

Եւ ահա իշխանութիւն առեալ չարասէր սպասաւորացն, զի զչորս զինուորսն ի բուն աւագացն մատուցեն ի փորձութիւն տանջանացն: Եւ զառաջեաւ դատեալ բազում հարուածովք, նովին կապանաւք անցուցին ի տեղիս արգելանին: Իսկ այլոցն խաբէութեամբ առ ժամանակ մի թողութիւն արարեալ, եւ զամենայն վնասուն պատճառս արկանէր զկապելովքն. եւ զայս առնէր սատանայական խրատուն:

Եւ յետ երկոտասան աւուրս հրաման տայր ընթրիս գործել առատութեամբ եւ աւելի քան զաւուրց սովորութիւն, եւ կոչէր զբազումս ի զինուորական քրիստոնէիցն: Եւ ի ժամ

But the soldiers cried out together with a beautiful thought and courageously said: "Heaven and earth are our witnesses that we have never been wanting in our duty to the king, nor have we ever confused cowardice with the strength of courage; these blows are vain and cruel."

This wailing resounded on every side until the king himself witnessed the proceedings with his own eyes, immediately made a vow and said: "I will not set you free until you fulfill my commands to my satisfaction."

And then his malicious servants received authority to subject four soldiers from among the natural *avag*s to tribulations and tortures. He started by condemning them with many beatings then threw them into prison bound in chains. He deceitfully remitted others for a time, putting all the blame of harm on the prisoners. He did this with Satanic direction.

After twelve days [of imprisonment] he gave orders for the preparation of an evening banquet, more sumptuous than ordinary, and invited many of the Christian soldiers. While the

գահուն պատրաստութեան զիւրաքանչիւր տեղի շնորհէր նոցա զբազմականին. եւ սիրով խոնարհութեամբ խաւսէր ընդ նոսա ըստառաջնում կարգին, զի թերեւս հաւանեսցին ուտել զմիս զոհեալ, զոր ոչ էր երբէք աւրէն ուտել քրիստոնէից: Իբրեւ ոչ կալան յանձին ամենեքին, ոչ ինչ կարի ստիպեաց, այլ հրամայեաց մատուցանել նոցա զսովորական կերակուրն, եւ առաւել գինեաւքն յաւելոյր ի տաճարին զխրախութիւն:

Եւ անտի ի դուրս ելեալ ի սրահն արքունի, արգելին զոմանս ի նոցանէ ձեռս յետս կապելով, եւ զխոնջանունսն կնքելով եւ զգուշութեամբ պահելով՝ էր որ զերկուս աւուրս, եւ էր որ զերիս: Բազում եւ այլ եւս յանարժան հարուածս չարչարէին, զոր եւ ոչ ընդ գրով իսկ արժանի համարեցաք արկանել: Եւ զոմանս ի նոցանէ հեռացուցին եւ քարշեցին յազնուական պատուոյն անարգեալ:

Եւ զունդս զունդս դարձեալ զումարէին ի նոցանէ յերկիր հեռաւոր `յամուրս անապատին՝ ի մարտ պատերազմի թշնամեացն արքայի. եւ բազմաց իսկ անդէն հասանէր վախճան մահու սրով: Եւ զամենեցուն զկարգեալ թոշակն նուազեցուցանէին, քաղցիւ եւ ծարաւով տառապեցուցանէին զնոսա, եւ ձմերոցի տեղիս զդժնեայ վայրսն հրամայէին նոցա. եւ անարգս եւ վատթարս յաչս ամենեցուն զնոսա ցուցանէին:

seating was being prepared, he graced each one with his own place at the table. He spoke with them with kind humility in accordance with their former rank, that he might prevail on them to eat sacrificial meat, of which the Christians were never permitted to eat.[20] When they all declined this, he did not force them, but ordered that their customary food be prepared for them, and increased the wine and feasting in the temple.

But when they were leaving the royal hall, some of the Christians were seized and arrested, and their pants sealed,[21] and they were held in close confinement; some for two days, and some for three. They were also demeaned in many other ways, which we will not deign to speak of here. Then some of them were sent away and deprived of their noble rank.

Then divisions upon divisions of soldiers were assembled from among them [the Christians] to march toward the deep wilderness in a distant land to fight the enemies of the king, where many of them perished by the sword. The wages [of the survivors] were reduced, they were tormented with famine and thirst, ordered to spend the winter in the cruelest of places and dishonored and vilified for all to see.

---

20 *i.e.*, meat offered to other deities or in the name of idolatry (cf. Acts 15:29).
21 A form of punishment in which one's pants are tied between the legs and around the bottom to retain urine and feces.

CHAPTER II

Իսկ նոքա առ սէրն Քրիստոսի յոյժ խնդութեամբ ընդունէին զամենայն չարչարանսն վասն մեծի յուսոյն, որ առաջի պատրաստեալ կայ պատուիրանապահ համբերողացն: Որչափ չարութիւն զանարգութիւն բազմացուցանէր, նոքա եւս քան զեւս զաւրանային ի սէրն Քրիստոսի. մանաւանդ զի բազումք ի նոցանէ զգիրս սուրբս ուսեալ էին ի մանկութենէ, զանձինս մխիթարէին եւ զընկերս քաջալերէին, եւ իբրեւ աշտարակ լուսոյ զպաշտաւնն ունէին եւ բազմացուցանէին:

Վասն որոյ եւ բազումք ի հեթանոսաց, որոց հեշտ եւ ցանկալի ձայնքն թուէին, քաջալերէին զնոսա, եւ ասէին բանս մխիթարութեան, իբրեւ թէ լաւիցէ մարդոյ մահու չափ ճգնել՝ քան յայդպիսի աւրինաց ուրանալ:

Բայց սակայն թէպէտ եւ նոքա առ սէրն Քրիստոսի յոյժ զուարթութեամբ խնդային ըստ ներքին մարդոյն, արտաքին տեսիլն կարի ողորմ էր յաւտարութեան: Այնպիսի պատուական զինուորութիւն հասեալ էր ի չարաշուք անարգութիւն, եւ հայրենի ազատութիւնն չարաչար կայր ի ծառայութեան մարդախոշոշ բռնաւորին, որ եւ ընդ հեթանոսաց աւրէնս անցանէր արհինհեղութեամբ, եւ ամենեւին չկարծէր՝ թէ գուցէ այսր ամենայն ի վրէժխնդիր յերկինս:

Նա եւ ոչ զերկրաւոր վաստակս ուրուք յիշէր. եւ որ մեծն քան զամենայն է ըստ մարմնաւոր կարգի, քանզի գոյին ոմանք ի նախարարացն, որոց զեղբարս նորա սնուցեալ էր մայրենի կաթամբն իւրեանց, առաւել եւս քան զամենեսեան զնոսա դատէր:

Yet out of their love of Christ, the Christians accepted all the torments with great joy and endured with the great hope of those who uphold the commandments. As much as evil multiplied dishonor, so much more were they strengthened in their love of Christ, especially because many of them had studied Holy Scripture from childhood and thus consoled themselves and encouraged their friends, performing and multiplying their worship like towers of light.

Thus many of the heathens, to whom the voices [of their songs] seemed pleasurable and desirous, began encouraging them and offering words of comfort, that it is better to bear deathly afflictions than to abjure such a religion.

However, although they were joyous in their love of Christ, their outer appearance was very pitiable compared to others. Such honorable soldiers had become objects of vile disrespect, and their ancestral noble rank was pitilessly subjected by their murderous captor, who followed the example of the bloodthirsty heathens who did not at all think that there could be vengeance for all this in heaven.

Also, no one remembered their earthly labor, which is above all else according to the mortal order, for some of the nakharars, whose brothers had been nourished with their mothers' milk, were tormented [by their brothers] more than anyone else.

Եւ յայսր ամենայնի վերայ այլ եւս չարութիւն խո-
րամանկեաց: Զմի ոմնի հաւատարիմ ծառայից իւրոց ի գործ
առաքէր յերկիրն Հայոց՝ որում անուն էր Դենշապուհ. որ
եկեալ հասեալ հրամանաւ արքունի, զողջոյն բերեալ զմեծ
թագաւորին, եւ խաղաղասէր կեղծաւորութեամբ աշխար-
հագիր առնել ամենայն երկրին Հայոց ի թողութիւն հար-
կաց եւ ի թեթեւութիւն ծանրութեան այրուձիոյն: Թէպէտ
եւ ի վերին երեսս կեղծաւորէր, այլ ի ներքոյ խորհուրդք
չարագոյն ցուցանէին:

Առաջին, զազատութիւն եկեղեցւոյն արկանէր ի ծառայութիւն:

Երկրորդ, միայնակեաց քրիստոնեայք որ բնակեալ
էին ի վանորայս, ընդ նովին աշխարհագրով էարկ:

Երրորդ, զհարկ աշխարհին առաւել ծանրացոյց:

Չորրորդ, զնախարարեանն բանսարկութեամբ արկ
ընդ միմեանս, եւ յամենայն տան արար խռովութիւն:

Եւ զայս ամենայն առնէր՝ թերեւս զմիաբանութիւնն
քակեսցէ, եւ զուխտն եկեղեցւոյն ցրուեսցէ, եւ զմիայնակ-
եացն փախուսցէ, եւ զշինականսն վատնեսցէ. եւ առ յոյժ
աղքատութեանն՝ ակամայ դիմեսցեն յաւրէնս մոգուց:

Եւ ե՛ւս չարագոյն հինգերորդն. քանզի որ հազարա-
պետն էր աշխարհին, իբրեւ զհայր վերակացու համարեալ
էր աշխարհականաց քրիստոնէից. գրգռեաց յարոյց զամ-
բաստանութիւն ի վերայ նորա, եւ հանեալ զնա ի գործոյն՝
փոխանակ նորա պարսիկած յաշխարհն, եւ մեւս եւս
մոգպետ՝ դատաւոր աշխարհին, զի զեկեղեցւոյն փառսն
աղաւաղեսցեն:

On top of all this, [the king] conspired to enact further wickedness. He sent one of his loyal servants named Denshapur to Armenia on an assignment. Denshapur arrived with a royal decree and the great king's greetings, and under a peaceful pretext he took a census of all of Armenia [with promises] to exempt them from paying taxes and to reduce burden on the cavalry. Although he concealed his artifice, the malice behind his plans was evident.

First, he turned the liberty of the church into servitude.

Second, he included the Christian monks who were living in monasteries in his census.

Third, he increased the taxes in the land.

Fourth, he slanderously pitched the nakharars against each other and established disorder in all their houses.

He did all this to try to destroy their unity, to break the brotherhood of the Church's faithful, and to put the monks to flight and exhaust the peasants, that they might, out of great poverty, turn to the Magian doctrine against their will.

Yet his fifth act was even more wicked: Given that the hazarbed of the land was considered as a father and overseer by its Christian inhabitants, Denshapur provoked accusations against him and removed him from his position, appointing a Persian to govern the land in his place and a mogbed as judge of the land to corrupt the glory of the church.

CHAPTER II

Բայց սակայն թէպէտ եւ ամենայն գործքս այս դժնեայ էին, չեւ էր ուրուք ձեռն արկեալ յայտնի յեկեղեցին. վասն այնորիկ եւ ոչ ոք ընդդիմացաւ նմա, թէպէտ եւ էր ծանրութիւն հարկացն: Քանզի ուստի արժան էր առնուլ հարիւր դահեկանաւ չափ, կրկին առնուին. նոյնպէս եւ եպիսկոպոսաց եւ երիցանց դնէին, ոչ միայն շինաց, այլ եւ աւերակաց: Նաեւ բնաւ ո՞վ իսկ կարէ պատմել վասն ծանրութեան մըտից եւ սակից, բաժից եւ հասից լերանց եւ դաշտաց եւ մայրեաց: Ոչ ըստ արքունի արժանաւորութեանն առնուին, այլ հինաբար յափշտակելով, մինչեւ ինքեանք իսկ մեծապէս զարմանային, թէ ուստի այս ամենայն գանձ ելանէ՝ զիա՞րդ շէն կայցէ աշխարհն:

Եւ իբրեւ տեսին՝ թէ այսու ամենայնիւ չկարացաք ձանձրացուցանել, յայնժամ յայտնապէս հրաման ետուն մոգաց եւ մոգպետաց նամակ մի գրել ըստ ձախողակի դենին իւրեանց:

Եւ է պատճէն նամակին այս.

Միհրներսեհ Վզուրկ հրամատար Երան եւ Աներան, Հայոց մեծաց ողջոյն շատ:

Դուք գիտասջիք, ամենայն մարդ՝ որ բնակեալ է ի ներքոյ երկնի, եւ ոչ ունի զաւրէնս դենի մազդեզն, նա խուլ է եւ կոյր, եւ ի դիւաց Հարամանոյ խաբեալ: Քանզի մինչ չեւ էին երկինք եւ երկիր, Զրուան մեծն աստուած յաշտ առնէր զհազար ամ եւ ասէր. «Թերեւս լիցի իմ որդի Որմիզդ անուն, արասցէ զերկին եւ զերկիր»:

But though all these works were foul, no man had lain a hand on the church openly; therefore, though the blows were heavy, no one opposed him. For when it was lawful to take 100 dahekans, they took double. They also did this with the bishops and priests, not only in populous areas, but also in desolate areas. Also, who could relate all the heavy taxes and levies, tolls and duties [imposed on the inhabitants of] the mountains, plains and forests? They did not take these according to the royal dignity; rather, they plundered like brigands until they themselves were astonished as to how the land could remain prosperous after they had taken all these treasures.

When they saw that even with all this, they could not trouble the Armenians, they openly ordered the magi and mogbeds to write a letter according to their sinister religion.

The following is a copy of this letter:

> *From Mihr Narseh, Grand Vizier of Eran and Aneran, abundant greetings to Greater Armenia.*
>
> *Know that all men who dwell beneath heaven and hold not the customs of the Mazdaean religion, are deaf and blind, and deceived by the demons of Ahriman. For before heaven and earth existed, the great god Zurvan made sacrifices for a thousand years and said: 'Perhaps I will have a son named Ormizd, who shall create heaven and earth.*

Եւ յղացաւ երկուս յորովայնի. մի վասն յաշտ առնելոյ՝ եւ զմեւսն եւս ի թերեւսն ասելոյ։ Իբրեւ գիտաց, եթէ երկու են յորովայնի, «Որ վաղ եկեսցէ, ասէ, նմա տաց զթագաւորութիւնս»։ Իսկ որ էր ի թերահաւատութենէն յղացեալ՝ պատառեաց զորովայնն եւել ի դուրս։ Ասէ ցնա Զրուան. «Ո՞վ ես դու»։ Ասէ. «Որդին քո եմ Որմիզդ»։ Ասէ ցնա Զրուան. «Իմ որդին լուսաւոր է եւ անուշահոտ, դու խաւարային ես եւ չարասէր»։ Եւ իբրեւ կարի դառնապէս ելաց, ետ ցնա զթագաւորութիւնն հազար ամ։

Իբրեւ ծնաւ զմեւս եւս որդի, անուանեաց զնա Որմիզդ. Եհան զթագաւորութիւն յԱրհմնէ, եւ ետ ցՈրմիզդն եւ ասէ ցնա. «Յայժմ ես քեզ յաշտ արարի, արդ դու ինձ արա». Եւ Որմիզդ արար զերկինս եւ զերկիր, իսկ Արհմն ընդդէմ չար գործեաց։

Եւ այսպէս բաժանին արարածքս. հրեշտակք Որմզդի են, իսկ դեւքն Արհմնոյն, եւ ամենայն բարիք, որ յերկնից եւ այսր լինին՝ Որմզդի են, եւ ամենայն վնասք, որ անտի եւ այսր գործին՝ զայն Արհմն արար։ Սոյնպէս յերկրիս որ ինչ բարի է՝ զայն Որմիզդն արար, եւ որ ոչն է բարի՝ զայն Արհմն արար. որպէս զմարդ Որմիզդ արար, եւ զախտս եւ զհիւանդութիւնս եւ զմահ Արհմն արար։ Եւ ամենայն թշուառութիւնք եւ պատահարք որ լինին, եւ պատերազմունք դառնութեան, չարին մասին արարածք են. իսկ յաջողութիւն եւ տէրութիւնք եւ փառք եւ պատիւք եւ առողջութիւնք մարմնոց, գեղեցկութիւնք դիմաց եւ ճարտարութիւնք բանից եւ երկայնակեցութիւնք ամաց, այդ ի բարւոյն առնուն զգոյացութիւն. եւ ամենայն որ ոչ այդպէս է, ի նա չարին արարած խառնեալ է։

Then he conceived two in his womb; one because of his sacrifice, and the other because he said 'perhaps'. When he learned that there were two in his womb, 'To whomever comes first,' he said, 'I shall bestow my kingdom.' Then the one who had been conceived of this doubt ripped his belly open and came out. Zurvan said to him: 'Who are you?' He said: 'I am your son Ormizd.' Zurvan said: 'My son is luminous and sweet-smelling; you are dark and malevolent.' Then, having wept very bitterly, Zurvan granted him sovereignty for a thousand years.

When his other son was born, he called him Ormizd; [Zurvan] then took sovereignty from Ahriman, gave it to Ormizd, and said to him: 'Until now I sacrificed to you; now, you must do the same to me.' Then Ormizd made heaven and earth while Ahriman wrought evil against him.

Thus, all creatures were divided: angels are of Ormizd and demons of Ahriman; all acts of good here and in heaven are Ormizd's, and all harms here and there are inflicted by Ahriman. And thus, whatever is good on this earth, Ormizd has made; and whatever is not good, Ahriman has made; just as Ormizd made man, so Ahriman made disease, illness and death. And all misfortunes, accidents, and bitter wars are the work of the evil side, just as prosperity, dominion, glory, honor, health of body, beauty of countenance, eloquence and longevity receive their existence from the good twin. All that is not so is mixed with the creation of the evil twin.

Եւ ամենայն մարդիկ մոլորեալ են, որ ասեն՝ եթէ «Զմահ Աստուած արար, եւ չար եւ բարի ի նմանէ լինին»: Մանաւանդ որպէս քրիստոնեայք ասեն՝ թէ Աստուած նախանձոտ է. վասն թզոյ միոյ ուտելոյ ի ծառոյն՝ Աստուած զմահ արար, եւ զմարդն էարկ ընդ այնու պատուհասիւ: Զայդպիսի նախանձ եւ ոչ մարդ առ մարդ ունի, թո՛ղ թէ Աստուած առ մարդիկ. զի որ զայս ասէ՝ նա խուլ է եւ կոյր, եւ ի դիւաց Հարամանոյ խաբեալ:

Դարձեալ մեւս եւս այլ մոլորութիւն. Աստուած որ զերկինս եւ զերկիր արար՝ եկն, ասեն, եւ ի կնոջէ ումեմնէ ծնաւ՝ որում անուն էր Մարիամ, եւ առն նորա Յովսէփ: Այլ ճշմարտութեամբ՝ Բանթուրական ուրումն եղեալ նա որդի յանկարգ խառնակութենէ: Եւ զհետ այսպիսի մարդոյ մոլորեալ են բա-զումք:

Եթէ աշխարհն Հոռոմոց առ յոյժ յիմարութեան ագիտաբար մոլորեալ են եւ զրկեալ ի կատարեալ դենէս մերմէ, յանձանց պարմայեն զվնասն իւրեանց. դուք եւս ընդէ՞ր զհետ նոցա մոլորութեանն ցնորիք: Այլ զոր աւրէնս տէրս ձեր ունի, զնոյն եւ դո՛ւք կալարուք. մանաւանդ զի եւ առաջի Աստուծոյ վասն ձեր համարս ունիմք տալ:

And all men err who say that 'God made death, and both evil and good are from Him.' Especially as the Christians hold that God is envious because man ate one fig from a particular tree, on account of which God made death and subjected man to the punishment of death. Not even man envies man in such a way, let alone God. So whoever says this is deaf and blind, and deceived by the demons of Ahriman.

And another error: They say that God, who made heaven and earth, came and was born of a woman whose name was Mary and whose husband was Joseph. The truth is that he was born of a man named Pantera, the son of an illegitimate intercourse. Afterwards, many people were led astray by this man.

If all of Rome has errantly deprived themselves of our perfect religion, they have brought it upon themselves out of their folly and ignorance. Why are you also deluded by their error? Whatever religion your sovereign holds, the same you must also take, especially because we have to account for you before God.

CHAPTER II

*Մի՛ հաւատայք առաջնորդացն ձերոց, զոր նած-
րացիսդ անուանէք. քանզի յոյժ են խաբեբայք. զոր
բանիւք ուսուցանեն, գործովք ոչ առնուն յանձն:
«Միս ուտել, ասեն, ոչ են մեղք», եւ ինքեանք ուտել
ոչ կամին. «Կին առնել արժան է», բայց ինքեանք
եւ հայել ի նա ոչ կամին. «Կարասի որ ժողովէ,
ասեն, մեղք են յոյժ», բայց զաղքատութիւն առաւել քան զյոյժ գովեն: Յարգեն զթշուառութիւն, եւ
պարսաւեն զյաջողուածս. ծաղր առնեն զանուն
բախտի, եւ զփառաւորութիւն յոյժ այպանեն. սի-
րեն զանշքութիւն հանդերձից, եւ յարգեն զանարգս քան զպատուականս. գովեն զմահ եւ պարսաւեն զկեանս. անարգեն զծնունդս մարդոյ եւ գովեն զանորդութիւն: Եւ եթէ լսէ ոք դոցա եւ ի կանայս ոչ մերձենան, աշխարհի վախճան վաղվաղակի հասանէ:*

*Այլ ես ոչ կամեցայ զամենայն ըստ մասանց ընդ
գրով արկանել առ ձեզ. զի բազում այլ ինչ է, զոր
խաւսին դոքա: Որ չարագոյն եւս է քան զոր գրե-
ցաքդ, զԱստուած ի խաչ ելեալ ի մարդկանէ քա-
րոզեն, եւ զնոյն մեռեալ եւ թաղեալ, եւ ապա յարուցեալ եւ վերացեալ յերկինս: Ո՞չ ահա ձեզէն իսկ
արժան էր անդէն դատաստան առնել վասն այդ-
պիսի անարժան ուսմանց: Դեւք որ չարք են, ոչ ըմ-
բռնին եւ տանջին ի մարդկանէ, թո՛ղ թէ Աստուած արարիչ ամենայն արարածոց. զոր ձեզ ա-
մաւթ է ասել, եւ մեզ կարի անհաւատալի բանք:*

*Արդ երկու իրք կան առաջի ձեր. կամ արարէք
բան առ բան նամակիդ պատասխանի, եւ կամ
արիք ի Դուռն եկայք, եւ յանդիման լերուք մեծի
հրապարակին:*

Do not believe your leaders whom you call Nazarenes, for they are very deceitful. What they teach in words, they do not perform in deeds. 'To eat meat,' say they, 'is not sin,' yet they do not wish to eat it; 'It is right to take a wife,' yet they do not wish to even look at women. 'Accumulating goods,' they say, 'is a great sin,' yet they praise poverty all the more. They honor misfortune and criticize success; they reproach fortune and mock glory; they love plainness of apparel and respect worthless things more than valuables; they praise death and condemn life; they degrade human births and praise childlessness. And if anyone should heed them and not approach women, the end of the world would shortly follow.

But I did not resolve to expound all this detail to you in writing, for there is much else that they say. Worse still than what we have related, they preach that God was crucified by man, and likewise that he died and was buried, and then rose and ascended to heaven. "Was it not suitable for you to pronounce a judgment about such unworthy teachings? Evil demons cannot be seized and tortured by men, let alone by God, the maker of all creatures. It is shameful of you to say this, and exceedingly unbelievable to us.

Now, there are two options before you; either respond to each point in this letter in writing, or come to the royal court and appear before the great assembly.

ԱՆՈՒԱՆՔ ԵՊԻՍԿՈՊՈՍԱՑՆ, որք ժողովեցան յԱյ-
րարատեան գաւառն եւ արարին նամակին պատասխանի.

ՅՈՎՍԷՓ եպիսկոպոս Այրարատոյ:
ՍԱՀԱԿ եպիսկոպոս Տարաւնոյ:
ՄԵՂԷՏ եպիսկոպոս Մանազկերտոյ:
ԵԶՆԻԿ եպիսկոպոս Բագրեւանդայ:
ՍՈՒՐՄԱԿ եպիսկոպոս Բզնունեաց:
ՏԱՃԱՏ եպիսկոպոս Տայոց:
ԹԱԹԻԿ եպիսկոպոս Բասենոյ:
ՔԱՍՈՒ եպիսկոպոս Տուրուբերանոյ:
ԵՐԵՄԻԱ եպիսկոպոս Մարդաստանի:
ԵՒՂԱՂ եպիսկոպոս Մարդոյաղւոյ:
ԱՆԱՆԻԱ եպիսկոպոս Սիւնեաց:
ՄՈՒՇԷ եպիսկոպոս Արծրունեաց:
ՍԱՀԱԿ եպիսկոպոս Ռըշտունեաց:
ԲԱՍԻԼ եպիսկոպոս Մոկաց:
ԳԱԴ եպիսկոպոս Վանանդայ:
ԵՂԻՇԱ եպիսկոպոս Ամատունեաց:
ԵՂԲԱՅՐ եպիսկոպոս Անձաւացեաց:
ԵՐԵՄԻԱ եպիսկոպոս Ապահունեաց:

Այս ամենայն եպիսկոպոսք եւ բազում քորեպիսկո-
պոսք եւ պատուական երիցունք ի տեղեաց տեղեաց հանդերձ սուրբ ուխտիւ եկեղեցւոյ՝ միաբանք եւ միահաւանք,
միահամուռ ժողովեալք ի թագաւորանիստ տեղին յԱրտա-
շատ, հաւանութեամբ մեծամեծ նախարարացն եւ ամենայն
բազմութեամբ աշխարհին արարին նամակին պատասխանի:

These are the names of the bishops who gathered in the province of Ayrarat and responded to the letter:

Hovsep, Bishop of Ayrarat.
Sahak, Bishop of Taron.
Meghet, Bishop of Manazkert.
Yeznik, Bishop of Bagrevand.
Surmak, Bishop of Bznunik.
Tachat, Bishop of Tayk.
Tatik, Bishop of Basen.
Kasu, Bishop of Turuberan.
Yeremia, Bishop of Mardastan.
Yevghagh, Bishop of Mardoyagh.
Anania, Bishop of Syunik.
Mushe, Bishop of the Artsrunik.
Sahak, Bishop of the Reshtunik.
Basil, Bishop of Mokk.
Gad, Bishop of Vanand.
Yeghisha, Bishop of Amatunik.
Yeghbayr, Bishop of Andzawatsik.
Yeremia, Bishop of Apahunik.

All these bishops, many chorbishops, venerable priests from various places and the holy clergy of the church collectively assembled at the royal residence in the city of Artashat, unanimously and of one accord, and at the desire of the most distinguished nakharars and of the whole multitude of the country, responded to the letter.

«ՅՈՎՍԷՓ ԵՊԻՍԿՈՊՈՍ, հանդերձ ամենայն միաբանելովքս ի մեծամեծաց մինչեւ ցփոքունս, Միհրներսեհի մեծի հազարապետի Արեաց եւ Անարեաց ՝ բազում խաղաղաւէր մտաւք բազմացի ողջոյն առ քեզ եւ ամենայն մեծի սպահիդ Արեաց.

Ի նախնեաց ունիմք սովորութիւն աստուածատուր պատուիրանաւ՝ աղաւթս առնել ի վերայ կենաց թագաւորի, եւ անձանձրոյթ խնդրել յԱստուծոյ վասն երկայն ժամանակաց դորա, զի խաղաղութեամբ վարեսցէ զտիեզերական իշխանութիւնդ, զոր աւանդեալ է դմա յԱստուծոյ. զի ի դորա յերկար խաղաղութեանն եւ մեք առողջութեամբ եւ աստուածպաշտութեամբ կատարեսցուք զկեանս մեր:

Վասն նամակին որ քո ի մեր աշխարհս տուեալ էր՝ առաջ ժամանակաւ մի ումն ի մոգպետաց, որ կատարելագոյն էր ի դենիդ ձերում, եւ դուք առաւել քան զբնութիւն մարդկան ի վեր համարէիք զնա, հաւատաց նա յԱստուած կենդանի՝ յարարիչն երկնի եւ երկրի, եւ բան առ բան ելոյծ եւ իմացոյց ձեզ զաւրէնս ձեր: Եւ իբրեւ ոչ կարացին բանիւ զդէմ ունել նորա, քարկոծեալ մեռաւ յՈրմըզդէ արքայէ: Եւ եթէ հաւատարիմ համարիցիս զմեր բանս լսել, ի բազում տեղիս այդր աշխարհիդ ձերոյ գտանին գիրք նորա. ընթերցիր, այտի տեղեկանաս:

Bishop Hovsep, in unison with all those who are in consent with us, both great and small, to Mihr Narseh, great hazarbed of the Aryans and non-Aryans. Abundant greetings in peace to you and the entire great army of the Aryans.

From our forefathers we have a custom, given by divine command, to pray for the life of the king, and to ceaselessly ask God to give him longevity that he may peacefully govern his universal dominion conferred upon him by God, and so that in his long peace, we may fulfill our lives in health and in the worship of God.

Regarding the letter you sent to our country, in former times one of your mogbeds, who was perfect in your religion, and whom you held to be above a mortal nature, believed in the living God, Creator of heaven and earth, and word by word he explained and informed you of your doctrine. But since they could not refute him, he was stoned to death by Hormizd the king. And if you should be so faithful as to hear our words, his books are to be found in many places in that country of yours: read, and you will be informed.

CHAPTER II

Այլ վասն աւրինացս մերոց, ոչ ինչ աներեւոյթ են, եւ ոչ յանկեան ուրեք աշխարհի քարոզի, այլ համատարած ընդ ամենայն երկիր, ընդ ծով եւ ընդ ցամաք եւ ընդ կղզիս. ոչ միայն ընդ արեւմուտս, այլ եւ ընդ արեւելս, այլ եւ ընդ հիւսիս եւ ընդ հարաւ եւ ի միջոցս լի է հոծութեամբ: Ոչ ի մարդ ապաստան՝ եթէ վերակացուաւ տարածեսցի ընդ աշխարհս. այլ ինքն յինքենէ ունի զհաստատութիւն: Ոչ առ այլովք վատթարաւքն վեհ երեւի, այլ ի վերուստ յերկնուստ ունի զանսուտ աւրէնըսդրութիւնն. ոչ միջնորդաւ, զի մի է Աստուած, եւ չիք այլ ոք բաց ի նմանէ, ոչ երիցագոյն եւ ոչ կըրսերագոյն:

Ոչ սկիզբն առեալ յումեքէ լինել Աստուած, այլ ինքըն ինքեամբ մշտնջենաւոր. ոչ ի տեղւոջ ուրեք, այլ ինքն ինքեան տեղի. ոչ ի ժամանակի իմիք, այլ ժամանակք ի նմանէ գոյացան. եւ ոչ միայն քան զերկինս երիցագոյն, այլ եւ քան զկարծիս մտաց մարդկան եւ հրեշտակաց: Ոչ ձեւանայ ի տեսիլ տարրեղէն, եւ ոչ անկանի ընդ տեսլեամբ ական. եւ ոչ միայն ձեռին չզննի, այլեւ ոչ ընդ միտս ուրուք հարկանի, ոչ միայն ընդ մարմնականացս, այլ եւ ընդ անմարմին հրեշտակացն. բայց եթէ ինքն կամի, իւրոց արժանաւորացն մտաց իմանի, այլ ոչ աչաց տեսանի. եւ մտաց՝ ոչ երկրաւորացս, այլ որ յԱստուած են հաւատացեալ ճշմարտի:

As for our religion, however, nothing is unclear, nor is it preached in some obscure corner of the land, but is spread over the whole earth, throughout the sea, the land, and even the islands; not only in the West, but also in the East, the North and the South, and densely in between. Not through the refuge of man did a protector spread Christianity through the land, but its firmness is in itself. It does not appear good by comparison with base things, but from the heavens above it has its unerring legislation, and not through any mediator, for God is one, and there is none other than Him, neither senior nor junior.

God did not receive beginning from anyone, but He is of Himself eternal; not in some place, but in His own place; not from any time, but all time comes from Him; and He is not only older than the heavens, but older also than the thoughts in the minds of men and angels. He does not take the form of the visible elements and is not perceptible to the eye; and not only can He not be felt by hand, but He also cannot be comprehended by the mind of any man—not only among corporeal [beings] but even among the bodiless angels; but if He wills, He will be known to the minds of the deserving, albeit not visibly to their eyes, and not to secular minds, but to those who truly believe in God.

Եւ անուն նորա Արարիչ երկնի եւ երկրի. իսկ յառաջ քան զերկին եւ զերկիր, որպէս ինքնագոյ՝ ինքնանուն է: Ինքն անժամանակ է, իսկ արարածոցս յորժամ կամեցաւ՝ սկիզբն արար լինելոյ, ոչ յընչէ այլ յոչընչէ. Զի ինչ՝ նա միայն է, եւ այլս ամենայն ի նմանէ ընչացաւ: Ոչ եթէ իբրեւ յետոյ իմացաւ եւ արար, այլ մինչ չեւ արարեալ էր նորա՝ ի կանուխ գիտութեանն իւրում տեսանէր զարարածս. որպէս եւ այժմ մինչ չեւ է գործեալ մարդոյ բարի ինչ կամ չար, Աստուծոյ յայտնի են գործք մարդկան: Սոյնպէս եւ յայնժամ մինչ չեւ էր արարեալ ոչ խառն ի խուռն ինչ ճանաչէր զանեղսն, այլ կարգեալ եւ յարմարեալ կային առաջի նորա իւրաքանչիւր մասանցն տեսակքն. Իսկ մարդկան եւ հրեշտակաց՝ եւ տեսակքն եւ որ ի տեսակին լինելոց էին:

Եւ քանզի արարող զաւրութիւն է, ոչ կարէր խափանել զնորա բարերարութիւնն մեր չարութիւնս. որպէս եւ եղեւ իսկ, եւ ունիմք դատաւոր զաջն արարիչ: Ձեռք որ զերկինս եւ զերկիր հաստատեցին, նոյն եւ տախտակս քարեղէնս փորագրեցին եւ ետուն մեզ դպրութիւն, որ ունի զաւրէնս խաղաղականս եւ փրկականս. զի գիտասցուք զմի Աստուած արարիչ երեւելեաց եւ աներեւութից. ոչ այլ եւ այլ, իբր թէ ումն բարի եւ ումն չար, այլ մի եւ նոյն համակ բարի:

His name is Creator of heaven and earth, and He was before heaven and earth, for He came into existence of Himself and is self-named. He is timeless, and gave beginning to existence when He willed it; not from something, but from nothing—for He alone is Being, and everything else came into being from Him. It was not after He came to know and created them, but before creating them that He in his foreknowledge had beheld His creatures. Just as now, before something good or evil is undertaken by man, the works of men are already known to God. So he also knew then, before He had created the uncreated beings—and not as some mishmash, but—by arranging and conforming before him each type of body part, both of men and angels, and of everything that would have a form.

And because He is a creative force, His beneficence could not obstruct our [acts of] evil; but as it turns out, we have a Judge on the right side of the Creator. The hands that established heaven and earth are the same ones that inscribed the stone tablets and brought us books containing the laws of peace and redemption, that we may know the one God, Creator of things visible and invisible; not disparately, as though one were good and another evil, but one and the same, and entirely good.

Բայց եթէ թուիցի քեզ չար ինչ գոլ յարարածս Աստուծոյ, ապա համարձակ, զի թերեւս ուցիս զճշմարիտն բարի: Ջհեւս չար ասացեր. գոն եւ դեւք բարի, զոր եւ դուք եւ մեք հրեշտակս անուանեմք. եթէ կամին՝ եւ դեւք բարի լինին, եւ եթէ կամին՝ եւ հրեշտակք չար լինին: Այդ եւ ի մարդիկ երեւի, եւ առաւել ի միոյ հաւր որդիս. է որ հնազանդ եւ հպատակ է հաւրն, եւ է որ չարագոյն քան զաստանայ: Նա եւ ինքն իսկ մարդն առանձին յերկուս բաժանեալ տեսանի, երբեմն չար եւ երբեմն բարի. եւ որ բարին էր՝ նոյն եւ չարացաւ, դէպ եղեւ, զի դարձեալ անդրէն ի բարին շրջեցաւ, եւ բնութիւն մի է:

Բայց այն որ ասեսն, եթէ վասն թզոյ միոյ մահ արար Աստուած, վատթարագոյն է պատառ մի մազաղաթ քան զթուզ. ապա եթէ բան թագաւորին նկարի ի նմա, ո պատառէ զնա, մահու ընդունի զպատուհաս: Իսկ արդ չար արժա՞ն է ասել թագաւորին. քաւ, ես ոչ ասեմ, այլ խրատ ի գործ արկեալ զայլս ուսուցանեմ: Յա՛յնժամ էր Աստուած նախանձոտ, թէ չէր պատուիրեալ չուտել ի ծառոյ անտի. ապա եթէ յառաջագոյն զգուշացաւ, զգութ բնական սիրոյն իւրոյ յայտնեաց ի նմա: Իսկ արհամարհելով մարդ՝ ընկալաւ զպատիժ մահուան:

But if it seems to you that there exists any evil within God's creatures, say it boldly, for you may come to learn of the true good. You called the devs evil, but there are also good devs, which you and we call angels—if they so resolve, demons can be good, and if they so resolve, angels can be evil. This appears also among people, and even among sons from the same father, as when one is obedient and acquiescent to him and the other more wicked than Satan. Also, each man himself appears to be divided in two, sometimes evil and sometimes good—he who is good turns evil, and when that happens, he returns again to good, yet his nature is one and the same.

But as for what you say about God having made death because of one fig, a piece of one parchment is even more worthless than a fig, yet if the words of the king are written on it, then the one who rips it is sentenced to death. Now, is it right to speak ill of the king? No, I say not; I only adduce this as an example with which to teach others. God would have only become jealous if He had not commanded them not to eat from that tree; in forewarning them, He showed His natural love and sympathy toward them. It is by scorning that, that man received the punishment of death.

Բայց այն զոր ասացեր՝ եթէ Աստուած ի կնոջէ ծնաւ, յայղմ չէր արժան քեզ խորշել եւ փախչել. զի անաւասիկ Արհմն եւ Որմիզդ ի հաւրէ ծնան եւ ոչ ի մաւրէ. որում եթէ քաջ միտ դնես, եւ ոչ դու յանձն առնուս: Եւ մեւս եւս այլ ծաղրագոյն քան զայդ, Միհր աստուած ի կնոջէ ծնանի, եթէ ոք ընդ իւրում ծնողին անկցի:

Այլ սակաւիկ մի եթէ ի բաց թողացուցանէիր զփիլ-քումն ուէրութեանդ, եւ ընկերաբար գայիր ի պայ-քար, գիտեմ զի իբրեւ այլովդ ամենայնիւ յոյժ իմաստուն ես, եւ վասն ծննդեան Տեառն մերոյ ի սուրբ Կուսէն՝ ոչ աւելաբանութիւն համարէիր, այլ առաւել քան զարարչութիւնն յոչընչէ զաշխարհս մեծագոյն զվերջին փրկութիւնն իմանայիր, ազա-տութեան մարդոյն զյանցաւորութիւնն դնէիր, եւ բարերարութեանն Աստուծոյ՝ զազատութիւնն ի ծառայութենէ:

Քանզի յորժամ լսես եթէ յոչընչէ արար Աստուած զամենայն աշխարհս բանիւ ծնունդ իմացիր զարարածս: Իսկ քանզի Աստուած, որ զայս մեծ մարմին առանց չարչարանաց ծնաւ, ապաքէն իբրեւ զհայր գութ ունի ընդ սմա: Զի որ ինքն անապական է, եւ զարարածս առանց ապակա-նութեան ծնաւ. իսկ սա կամաւք գլորեալ ապա-կանեցաւ, եւ անձամբ եւս ոչ կարէր կանգնել կա-լի վերայ ոտից: Վասն զի էր ի հողոյ, անձամբ անձին արարեալ՝ անդրէն ի նոյն բնութիւն դար-ձաւ. եւ իբրեւ ոչ եթէ յաւտար զաւրութենէ չարի ինչ ընկալաւ ուրուք զպատիժս պատուհասին, այլ ի յիւրմէ հեղգութենէն չլսել բարերար պատուիրա-նին, խրատեցաւ ծառայական մասնն մահուամ-բըն, զոր կրեաց յանձն իւր:

But regarding what you said, that God was born of a woman, it was not fitting for you to turn away from that point; for behold, Ahriman and Ormizd were born of a father and not of a mother, to which, if you apply all your reasoning, you would still not be able to grasp. And even more risible than that, the god Mihr was born of a woman, as though someone would lie with his own parent.

But if you would set aside the pride of your authority for a little while and engage in amicable debate, I know that you are very wise in other matters and did not consider the birth of our Lord from the Holy Virgin as superfluous, and that you understand the Last Judgment to be greater than the creation of the world out of nothing, and that you attribute the transgression to man's liberty and his freedom from service to God's beneficence.

For when you hear that God made this entire world out of nothing, consider that all things in the world were born by His word. And so God, who created this great body without suffering, has compassion for it as a father. And as He is incorruptible, so too His creatures were born without corruption. But the latter fell into corruptibility of its own volition, and could no longer stand on its own feet by itself. And being made of dust, he returned to the same nature—not through some foreign evil power did they fall into the punishment of death, but through their own negligence, by not heeding the good commandment. Thus their servile part was punished with death, which each person bore in himself.

Արդ եթէ զմահ չար աստուածն արար, զի՞նչ գոյացութիւն երեւի մահուի միջի. եւ ո՛չ ինչ: Բայց զբարի Աստուծոյ զարարածսն խանգարեաց: Եթէ այդ այդպէս է, նմա եւ բարի իսկ ասել ոչ մարթի, այլ կիսագործ ապականացու: Եւ որոյ աստուծոյ արարածքն ապականելիք են եւ եղծանելիք՝ նմա անեղծ Աստուած չմարթի ասել: Տի՛ աւն անդըր թողէք զյիմարութեան զբարբանջմունսդ:

Միոյ աշխարհի երկու դեհապետք ոչ լինին, եւ ոչ միոյ արարածոյ երկու աստուածք: Եթէ ժպրհեսցին եւ լինիցին երկու թագաւորք միոյ աշխարհի, աշխարհն եղծանի եւ թագաւորութիւնքն խանգարին:

Աշխարհս նիւթեղէն է, եւ նիւթքս որիշ որիշ են եւ ընդ միմեանս հակառակ. մի է արարիչ հակառակորդացս, որ ածէ զոսսա ի սիրելութիւն հաւանութեամբ. որպէս մալեալ կակղէ զջերմութիւն հրոյն՝ աւդոյս հովութեամբ, եւ զապառումն բրտութիւն աւդոյն՝ հրոյս եռանդմամբ. սոյնպէս եւ զմանրամաղ փոշիացեալ հողս՝ ջրոյս խոնաւութեամբ զանգանէ, իսկ զ'ի վայր ծորելի բնութիւն ջրոյն՝ սալայատակ տրտմացեալ հողոյս կափմամբ:

Now if the evil god has created death, then what substance appears from death? None! For death destroys the creatures of the good God. Now if this is so, then these cannot be called good, but imperfect and corruptible, and the god whose creatures are corruptible and destructible cannot be called incorruptible God. Now, then, give up your blathering!

One land does not have two rulers, nor does one creature have two gods. If two kings dared to rule over one land, their kingdoms would fall into disorder and the land would be ruined.

The world is material, and the material [elements] are distinct and in opposition to one another. The Creator of these opposing elements is One, who brings them into affection through harmony. As He crushes and softens the heat of the fire through the coolness of air and the harshness of the cold air with the warmth of fire, so too does He pulverize the earth into tiny pieces and cast the moisture of water down, and the nature of water flows downwards to be hardened by the binding of the earth.

*Զի եթէ միաբանէին տարերքս, գուցէ որք ի կար-
ճամտաց եւ Աստուած անապական զոսա կարծէր, եւ թողեալ զարարիչն՝ արարածոցս զերկըր-
պագութիւն մատուցանէր. վասն այնորիկ որ ա-
րար զսա՝ զգուշացաւ յառաջագոյն, զի հայեցեալ
մարդիկ ի յանդիմանութիւն ապականացու տա-
րերցս՝ անապական միայն զկառավար սորա ի-
մացին, զմի եւ ոչ զերկուս. զնոյն արարիչ չո-
րեքկին նիւթոցս, յորմէ ամենայնքս ծննդագոր-
ծին հրամանաւ արարողին իւրեանց:*

*Եւ շրջագայութեամբք չորիւք յեղանակաւք կա-
տարեալ գործեն զտարեւոր սպասաւորութիւնն.
եւ չորեքեան հային կամաց ակնարկելոյ արար-
չին իւրեանց, եւ անզգայութեամբ լծեալ են ի
գործ հարկաւորութեան, չյափշտակելով զկարգ
պատուոյն ի միմեանց:*

*Եւ ահա պարզաբար ասացեալ դիւրատար լու-
սաւորութիւն յականջս ամենեցուն:*

*Զի այն որ հուրն է, գոյացութեամբ եւ զաւրու-
թեամբ խառնեալ է յերիսեւս մասունս. իբրեւ
զտանի ջերմութիւնն յոլովագոյն ի քարինս եւ
յերկաթս, եւ սակաւագոյն ի յաւդ եւ ի ջուր, եւ
ինքն առանձին ուրեք ոչ երեւի: Իսկ ջրոյ բնութիւն
գոյ առանձինն, գոյ եւ ի խառնուածսն երից եւս
մասանց, յոլովագոյն ի հողաբոյսս եւ սակաւագոյն ի յաւդ եւ ի հուր: Իսկ աւդն թափանցանց
է ընդ հուրն եւ ընդ ջուրն, եւ ի ձեռն ջրոյն ընդ
կերակուրս աճեցականս:*

For if these elements became united, perhaps some short-witted individual would think these formed an incorruptible god, and abandoning the Creator, would offer worship to His creatures instead. Hence, He who made all this observed in advance, that when man would see the opposition of these corruptible elements, he would only understand the Driver as incorruptible, and that He is one and not two—the same Creator of these four elements, from whom all works of creation are made.

The four seasons in their cycle fulfill their annual service, and all four look to the will and glance of the Creator, and are insentiently yoked to their indispensable work without seizing the established order from each other.

Now for a simple explanation that is easily comprehensible to the ears of all!

For that which is fire is, in substance and power, mixed with three other parts; as heat is found abundantly in stone and iron, less so in air and water, and never by itself. And the nature of water is such that it exists of itself, and in mixture with three other parts—more so in plants, and less so in air and in fire. But air penetrates fire and water, and through water, vegetal foods.

Եւ այսպէս խառնեալ են տարերքս այս, եւ գոյացեալ իբրեւ զմի մարմին, եւ ոչ կորուսեալ զիւրաքանչիւր բնութիւնս, եւ ոչ երբէք զկայան առեալ հակառակութեամբ, հայելով ի մի իշխանն յանխառնն, որ զխառնուածն յարմարեալ կազմէ առ ի բնակութիւն կենդանեաց ամենեցուն, եւ տեւողութիւն յարակայութեան բոլոր աշխարհիս:

Իսկ եթէ առ անբան աշխարհս այսպէս հոգ տանի Աստուած, ո՛րչափ եւս առաւել առ բանաւոր աշխարհն՝ մարդս:

Զոր եւ ձեր ումն քաջ յիմաստնոցն ասաց, եթէ Միհրն աստուած մայրածին էր ի մարդկանէ, եւ թագաւոր աստուածազաւակ է, եւ համհարզ քաջ եւթներորդաց աստուածոց: Եւ եթէ հաւատալ արժան է առասպելաբանութեանդ, զոր դուք եւ գործովք իսկ կատարեալ ցուցանէք ի դենիդ ձերում, մեք ոչ եւս առասպելացն հաւատամք, այլ աշակերտք եմք մեծին Մովսիսի մարգարէին, ընդ որում Աստուած խաւսեցաւ ի մորենւոջն ի Սինէ, եւ դէմ յանդիման աւրէնս գրեաց եւ ետ նմա. եւ ծանոյց զնիւթեղէն աշխարհս իբրեւ զարարածս, եւ զիւր աննիւթ էութիւնն՝ արարիչ նիւթոցս յոչընչէ. եւ զերկիրս երկրաւորաւքս եւ զերկինս երկնաւորաւք ծանոյց նմա, զի գործք ձեռաց նորա են: Բնակիչք երկնի՝ հրեշտակք, եւ բնակիչք երկրի՝ մարդիկ. բանաւոր՝ մարդ եւ հրեշտակ միայն, եւ Աստուած ի վեր քան զերկինս եւ զերկիր:

And thus the elements are mixed and combined as one body; neither do these lose their natures, nor do they ever take rest from opposing each other, looking to the one, pure Lord, who adjusts and forms their mixtures according to the nature of all living things, and to the perpetuity of the whole world.

Now if God takes such care of this irrational world, how much more so of the mortals of the rational world!

As for what one of your wisest men said, namely that the god Mihr was born of a mortal mother, a king born of god, and a brave adjutant of the seven gods. Now if it is right to believe this fable—which you set forth in your religion as flawless—well, we do not believe in fables, but are disciples of the great prophet Moses, with whom God conversed at the bush on Sinai, and to whom He wrote and delivered His laws to face to face. He taught him about the material world as creation and about his immaterial existence as the Creator of matter from nothing, and that the earth with its earthly creatures and the heavens with its heavenly beings are works of His hands. The inhabitants of heaven are angels, and the inhabitants of earth are men; men and angels alone are rational, with God above heaven and earth.

Եւ ամենայն արարածք անբանութեամբ կատարեն զհրամանս պատուիրանի նորա, եւ ոչ երբէք անցանեն ըստ եղեալ սահմանն իւրեանց. Բայց մարդ եւ հրեշտակ ազատ թողեալ ի կամս անձին, քանզի մտաւորք են, եթէ կայցեն ի հրամանի նորա, անմահք են եւ որդիք Աստուծոյ: Զբոլոր արարածս տուեալ է ի ծառայութիւն, զերկիրս՝ մարդկան, եւ զերկինս՝ հրեշտակաց. ապա եթէ ստունգանիցեն եւ անցանիցեն զպատուիրանաւ, զընդդէմսն գործեսցեն Աստուծոյ, յիւրաքանչիւր պատուոցն զանարգանս ընկալցին. զի երեւեսցի տէրութիւնն անբամբաս, եւ յանցաւորք յանցանացն ամաւթալից:

Իսկ եթէ դու ի տգիտութեան վրիպեալ ես, ես որ հաստատունս գիտեմ, ոչ կարեմ գալ զկնի քո մոլորութեանդ: Եթէ աշակերտիմ անուսմնութեանդ, երկոքինս յանգիտ կորուստն մատնիմք, թերեւս ես չարագոյն քան զքեզ, քանզի վկայ ունիմ ինձ զինքնասաց ձայնն Աստուծոյ. «Ծառայ, սաէ, որ ոչ գիտէ զկամս տեառն իւրոյ, եւ արժանի զանի ինչ գործ գործէ, ըմպել ըմպէ գան, այլ սակաւագոյն» իսկ որ տեղեկագոյն է կամաց թագաւորին, եւ յանցանէ ինչ առաջի նորա, առանց բարեխաւսի բազմապատիկ տանջի:

All creatures obey His command without reason and never do they overstep the limits prescribed to them. Only men and angels were given free will, for they possess reason, and if they live according to His command then they are immortal, and sons of God. But all creatures are given for servitude; earth to men, and heaven to angels, and if they do not heed and keep the commandment, they work against God and shall be deprived of all honor. For His dominion shall appear irreproachable and transgressors shall be shamed for their transgressions.

Now if you have been misled out of ignorance, I, being firm in my knowledge, cannot follow your error. For if I became a student of your ignorance, we should both be delivered into irredeemable destruction, and perhaps I worse than you, for I have as witness God's own voice: 'A servant,' He says, 'who does not know his master's will and is worthy of a beating, will be beaten less' and he who is well-informed of the king's will and does wrong before him is severely punished without intercession.'[22]

22 Luke 12:47-48.

CHAPTER II

Արդ աղաչեմ զքեզ եւ զամենեսեան, որ ընդ քոյով
իշխանութեամբ են. մի՛ դու ընդ իս բազմապատիկ
տանջիր, եւ ոչ ես ընդ քեզ սակաւագոյն. այլ ես եւ
դու եւ ամենայն բազմութիւնդ հանդերձ արի թա-
գաւորաւդ այնպէս աշակերտեսցուք աստուածային գրոց, զի ի տանջանացն ապրեսցուք, եւ զդը-
ժոխս արհամարհեսցուք, եւ յանշէջ հրոյն զերծա-
նիցիմք, եւ զարքայութիւնն ժառանգիցեմք, եւ
անցաւոր կենաւքս զանանց մեծութիւնն անվախ-
ճան ունիցիմք: Բայց յորմէ դուդ զարհուրեալ ես՝
դիւրահաւան լեր, եւ վաղվաղակի աշակերտիս ճշմարտութեանն:

Ումն ի հրեշտակաց յանմահիցն գնդէն ստամբակեալ եւ ի բաց գնացեալ յերկնից, եւ ի մեր
աշխարհս եկեալ՝ պատիր բանիւք եւ սուտ խոստ-
մամբ զանլինելի յոյսն առաջի դնէր՝ իբրեւ տղայ
մանկան՝ անփորձ եւ անկիրթ նորաթեք մարդոյն,
ի վեր հայեցուցանելով զմիտս նորա, ուտելով ի
պտղոյ ծառոյն, յոր հուպն չհրամայեաց երթալ,
զի լիցի աստուած: Իսկ նորա մոռացեալ զպատ-
ուիրանն Աստուծոյ, խաբեցաւ զկնի մոլար խաբէութեանն, կորոյս զոր ունէր զփառս անմահու-
թեանն, եւ չեհաս երազայոյս կարծեացն: Վասն ո-
րոյ եւ մերժեալ ի կենաց տեղւոյն, ընկեցաւ յա-
պականելի աշխարհս, յորում եւ դուք էք բնակեալ
այժմ, եւ ցնորեալ մոլորիք զկնի նորին խրատ-
տուի. ոչ եւս ուտելով ի պատուիրեալ ծառոյն, այլ
զարարածս աստուած ասելով, եւ անխաւս տա-
րերցս երկիր պագանելով, եւ անորովայն դիւաց
կերակուր մատուցանելով, եւ յարարչէն բոլորեցունց ի բաց լինելով:

Thus, I pray to you and to all who are under your rule: do not be greatly tormented with me, nor I less so with you; but that you and I and all the people in your valiant kingdom become disciples of the Divine Scripture, that we may escape torments, scorn hell, deliver ourselves from the unquenchable fire, inherit the kingdom, and attain eternal greatness in this transitory life. But as for that which troubles you, be willing to yield, and you will learn the truth quickly.

One from the legion of immortal angels left heaven in rebellion and came to our earth, and with enticing words and false promises put forth impracticable hope to an inexperienced, uneducated and newly created man, as though to a boy, turning his attention upwards in rebellion, so that, by eating the fruit of the tree—which he was forbidden to approach—he would become god. Now having forgotten the command of God, he was deceived by that errant fraud, and lost the glory of immortality which he had possessed so that he did not attain the hope of his dreams. Therefore, driven out of the place of life, he fell into this corruptible world, which you also now inhabit, and in which you now senselessly err following the same counselor: Not by eating of the forbidden tree, but by calling creatures god, worshipping voiceless elements, offering food to the demons without bellies, and renouncing the Creator of everything.

*Ոչ յագի չար խրատուն, այլ կամի, զի քան զին-
քըն չարագոյնս արասցէ: Քանզի դեւքն ոչ եթէ
բռնաբար զոք վարեն ի կորուստ, այլ զմեղս
քաղցրացուցանեն ի կամս մարդոյն, եւ ողոքա-
նաւք որսան զանուամունս ի խաբէութիւն, որպէս
բազում մարդիկ զընկերս իւրեանց ի գողութիւն
եւ յաւազակութիւն. իբր ոչ եթէ բռնի ինչ վարե-
լով, այլ պատիր խաբէութեամբ տան գործել բազում չարիս, զոմանս ի կախարդութիւն, եւ զոմանս ի պոռնկութիւն, եւ զոմանս յանթիւ ի բազում յայլ իրս աղտեղութեան: Եւ արդար դատա-
ւորաւք վրէժ առնուն մահու չափ. իբր ոչ եթէ
բարի Աստուծոյ դատաւորք իցեն բարեգործ, եւ
չարին չարագործ. զի բազում անգամ է՝ զի ի բարի
մարդկանէ չարք լինին, եւ յետոյ ի չարագունից
անտի կատարելագոյն բարիք:*

*Եւ դատաւորք ստոյգ, որք դատին զչարագործս,
ոչ եթէ չարք անուանին եւ չարչարիչք, այլ յոյժ
բարիք եւ բարեգործք. եւ բնութիւն մի է, եւ ոչ երկու. իսկ ի միջոջէ անտի գործք երկուութեան ե-
րեւին, ոմանց սատակիչք, եւ ոմանց պարգեւա-
տուք: Եւ եթէ առ մարդիկ այս պաշտի ի ձեռն
թագաւորական վիճակին խրատուն խնամ տանել իւրում իշխանութեանն, ո՞րչափ եւս առաւել
Աստուծոյ բոլոր աշխարհս, որ ընդ ամենեցուն
կեանս կամի եւ ոչ զմահ: Եւ ահա ուր բազմացաւ
յանցաւորութիւն, տանջեաց զամենեսեան մահուամբ. իսկ ուր եղեւ ունկնդրութիւն հնազանդու-
թեան, շնորհեաց զպարգեւս անմահութեան:*

The wicked counselor was not satisfied but resolved to do worse, for the demons cannot forcefully take anyone into destruction. So they sweeten sin to the will of man and capture the unlearned with flattery and artifice, in the same way that many people exhort their friends into theft and robbery: Not capturing them by force, but instead delivering them into working many kinds of evil by enticing trickery—some to sorcery, some to prostitution, and others into diverse impurities. Through just judges they receive death as revenge, and not because the judges of the good God are good and those of the evil [god] are evil; for very frequently evil comes from good men, and then the greatest good from the most evil men.

True judges who judge malefactors are not called evil or tormentors, but are called good and benefactors. Their nature is one, and not two-fold, yet from that one nature appear two types of deeds: for some, destructive, and for others, beneficial. And if mortal judges protect the kingdom by punishment through royal authority, how much more does God—who wills that all have life and not death—protect the whole world? Thus wherever transgressions multiplied, He tormented with death; and where there was earnest obedience, He granted the reward of immortality.

CHAPTER II

Այն է ճշմարիտ Աստուած՝ բոլորեցունց մեր արարիչ, զոր դու աներասանակ արձակ բերանով անահ աներկիւղ համարձակութեամբ հայհոյես: Թողեալ զՅիսուս Քրիստոս զփրկական անունն՝ Փանդուրակայ որդի անուանես, եւ մարդ մոլորեցուցիչ կարծես. եւ զերկնաւոր փրկութիւնն աղաւաղես եւ անարգես ի կորուստ անձին եւ բոլոր աշխարհիս: Զոր տալոց եւ հատուցանելոց ես զանանցական վրէժ տանջանացն յանշէջ հուրն սպառնացեալ գեհենին, հանդերձ ամենայն գործակցաւք քովք, առաջնովք եւ միջնովք եւ վերջնովք:

Այլ մեք այսպէս գիտեմք զԱստուած, եւ ի սոյն հաւատամք յաներկբայս:

Աստուած, որ արար զաշխարհս, նոյն եկն եւ ծնաւ ի սուրբ կուսէն Մարիամայ, յառաջագոյն նրկատելով մարգարէիցն, առանց իրիք պատճառանաց մարմնաւոր կարգի: Որպէս յոչընչէ արար զայս մեծ մարմին աշխարհս, սոյնպէս առանց իրիք մարմնական միջնորդի առ զմարմինն յանփորձ կուսէն ճշմարտիւ, եւ ոչ ստուերագիր երեւմամբ: Էր Աստուած ճշմարտիւ, եւ եղեւ մարդ ճշմարտիւ. ոչ ի լինելն մարդ՝ կորոյս զաստուածութիւնն, եւ ոչ ի կալ մնալն Աստուած՝ աղաւաղեաց զմարդկութիւնն, այլ նոյն եւ մի:

That is the true God, Creator of us all, Whom you, with unrestrained and loose mouth, undauntedly and fearlessly revile. Abandoning the name of the Savior Jesus Christ, you call Him the son of Pantera, and a deceiver of men; and you corrupt and dishonor heavenly redemption, destroying yourself and all the land, for which you will suffer endless revenge in the inextinguishable fire of hell with all your accomplices—the first, the middle and the last.

But this is how we know God, and in the same we believe without question:

God, who created the world, himself came and was born of the Holy Virgin Mary, as previously indicated by the prophets and without cause of mortal order. Just as He created this great body of the world out of nothing, so without any physical mediator He became truly embodied from the chaste Virgin. Not as a shadowy appearance, for He was truly God and truly became man. Not by becoming man did He lose godliness, nor by becoming and remaining God did He corrupt His manhood; but He was the same, and one.

*Այլ քանզի ոչ կարէաք տեսանել զանտեսանելին
եւ մերձենալ յանմերձենալին, եկն եմուտ ընդ մե-
րով մարդկութեամբս, զի եւ մեք մտցուք ընդ նորա աստուածութեամբն: Ոչ անարգանս ինչ հա-
մարեցաւ զգենուլ զիւր ստեղծուած մարմինս, այլ
մեծարեաց իբրեւ զաստուածաստեղծ զիւր գործ:
Ոչ առ սակաւ սակաւ շնորհեաց ինչ սմա զանմա-
հութեան պատիւն՝ իբրեւ զանմարմին հրեշտակաց, այլ միանգամայն զբոլոր բնութիւնն մարմնով, շնչով եւ հոգւով զգեցաւ, եւ միաբանեաց
ընդ աստուածութեանն. միութիւն, եւ ոչ երկուու-
թիւն. եւ այսուհետեւ մի գիտեմք զաստուածութիւնն, որ յառաջ էր քան զաշխարհս, նոյն եւ
այսաւր:*

*Այս Յիսուս Քրիստոս, որ յիւր մարմինն փրկեաց
զբոլոր աշխարհս, սա եկն կամաւ ի մահ. եւ որպէս ինքն աստուածութիւնն գիտէ՝ թանձրացաւ
յանարատ կուսէն, եւ ծնաւ եւ պատեցաւ ի խան-
ձարուրս եւ եդաւ ի մսուր, եւ շարժեաց էած
զմոգսն յարեւելից յերկրպագութիւն. սնաւ իբրեւ
զտղայ կաթամբ, աճեաց եւ մեծացաւ ամս երեսուն մկրտեցաւ ի Յովհաննէ ի յամլորդւոյն ի
Յորդանան գետ: Արար նշանս մեծամեծս եւ ար-
ուեստս ի մէջ Հրէիցն. մատնեցաւ ի քահանայից,
դատապարտեցաւ ի Պիղատոսէ Պոնտացւոյ: Խաչեցաւ, մեռաւ, թաղեցաւ, յարեաւ յաւուր երրորդի.
երեւեցաւ երկոտասան աշակերտացն եւ այլոց
բազմաց աւելի քան զհինգ հարիւրոցն: Եւ շրջելով
ընդ նոսա զաւուրս քառասուն՝ վերացաւ ի լեռնէն
Ձիթենեաց յերկինս յանդիման իւրոց աշակերտացն, եւ եւ նստաւ ի հայրենի աթոռն:*

But because we could not see the invisible and approach the unapproachable, He entered our humanity, that we may enter His divinity. He did not consider it as shameful to don this created body, but glorified His creation as divine. Nor did He little by little bestow the honor of His immortality, as the bodiless angels, but He put on all nature at once with body, breath and spirit, and united it with His divinity—as One, and not two. Thus have we come to know the One divinity, Who preceded the world and is the same today.

This Jesus Christ, who from His embodiment redeemed the whole world, came by His own will to die. Knowing divinity, He was formed from the unspotted virgin, was born, wrapped in swaddling clothes, laid in a manger, and drew the magi from the East to worship Him. He was nourished with milk as a boy, grew and came to age for thirty years and was baptized by John, the son of a barren woman, in the river Jordan. He performed great signs and miracles among the Jews, was betrayed by the priests, and was condemned by Pontius Pilate. He was crucified, dead, buried, and arose on the third day; He appeared to the twelve disciples and to many others—more than five hundred. He spent among them forty days, and then ascended from the Mount of Olives to heaven in the presence of His disciples, and rose and sat upon the throne of His Father.

CHAPTER II

Խոստացաւ երկրորդ անգամ գալ ահաւոր զաւ-րութեամբ յարուցանել զմեռեալս, նորոգել զբոլոր աշխարհս, առնել դատաստան արդար ի մէջ արդարոց եւ մեղաւորաց, տալ պարգեւս արժա-նաւորաց, եւ հատուցանել պատիժս չարագոր-ծաց, որ այսմ ամենայնի բարերարութեանց ոչ հաւատան:

Յայսմ հաւատոց զմեզ ոչ ոք կարէ խախտել, ոչ հրեշտակք եւ ոչ մարդիկ, ոչ սուր եւ ոչ հուր, ոչ ջուր, ոչ ամենայն զինչ եւ են դառն հարուածք:

Ամենայն ինչք եւ ստացուածք մեր ի ձեռս քո, եւ մարմինք մեր առաջի քոկան. ըստ կամաց քոց արա զինչ եւ կամիս: Եթէ սովին հաւատովք թո-ղուս, ոչ յերկրի այլ տէր փոխանակեմք ընդ քեզ, եւ ոչ յերկինս այլ Աստուած փոխանակեմք ընդ Յիսուսի Քրիստոսի, որ չիք այլ Աստուած բաց ի նմանէ:

Ապա եթէ յետ այսր մեծի վկայութեան այլ ինչ հարցանես, ահաւասիկ կամք զբոլոր մարմինս տու-եալ ի ձեռս քո. վաղվաղակի արա զինչ եւ կամիս: Ի քէն տանջանք եւ ի մէնջ յանձնառութիւնք. սուր քո՝ եւ պարանոցք մեր: Չեմք ինչ լաւ մեք քան զա-ռաջինսն, որ յայսր վկայութեան վերայ եդին զին-չս եւ զստացուածս եւ զմարմինս իւրեանց:

He promised to appear a second time with fearsome power and raise the dead, renew the world, execute true judgment among the righteous and sinful, to reward the worthy and punish the malefactors who believe not in all these benefactions.

No one can remove us from this faith, neither angels nor men, neither sword nor fire, nor water, nor any cruel beatings.

All our goods and possessions are in your hands, and our bodies are before you. Do what you will. If you allow us our own faith, we shall not trade you for any other lord on earth, nor in heaven shall we exchange for another god Jesus Christ, for there is no other God except Him.

Now if you should have any questions following this great testimony, see here that we resolve to put our bodies in your hands, so do with them what you will: Torture by you, acceptance from us. The sword is yours, the neck is ours. We are nothing better than our forefathers, who upon this testimony surrendered their goods and possessions and bodies.

Զի եթէ անմահք իսկ էաք, եւ մարթ էր մեզ մեռա-նել վասն սիրոյն Քրիստոսի, արժան էր. քանզի եւ նա անմահ էր, եւ ա՛յնչափ սիրեաց զմեզ, մինչեւ մահ ի յանձն էառ, զի եւ մեք նորա մահուամբն յաւիտենական մահուանէն ապրեսցուք: Եւ եթէ նա յիւր անմահութիւնն ոչ խնայեաց, մեք զի կա-մաւք եղաք մահկանացուք, կամաւք մեռցուք վասն սիրոյ նորա, զի կամաւք յանձն առցէ զմեզ յիւր յանմահութիւնն. մեռցուք իբրեւ զմահկանա-ցուս. զի ընկալցի զմեր մահն իբրեւ զանմահից:

Այլ դու յետ այսր ամենայնի այլ զմեզ մի՛ հարցա-ներ. զի ոչ եթէ ընդ մարդոյ է ուխտ հաւատոց մե-րոց, եթէ պատրիցիմք իբրեւ զտղայս. Այլ անլու-ծութեամբ ընդ Աստուծոյ, որում չիք հնար քակ-տել եւ ի բաց ելանել, ոչ այժմ եւ ոչ յապա, եւ ոչ յաւիտեանս, եւ ոչ յաւիտենից յաւիտեանս»:

Ի սմին մեծի հաւանութեան ամենայն բազմութիւնն միաբանեաց ի մեծամեծաց մինչեւ ցփոքունս. անսուտ երդ-մամբ եդին վկայութիւն՝ կենաց եւ մահու ի նմին կալ հաստատուն:

Եւ իբրեւ եհաս նամակն յարքունիս, եւ ընթերցան ի մեծի խոնաստանի յանդիման ամենայն բազմութեան կա-րաւանին, բազումք այնոքիկ էին, որ իբրեւ լսէին՝ գովէին զպատասխանիսն: Թէպէտ եւ երկնչէին յահէ տէրութեանն, սակայն ի ծածուկ առ միմեանս զնոյն վկայութիւնս գովու-թեանց տային. առաւել քան ընդ ճարտարաբանութիւնն՝ ընդ համարձակութիւն աներկիւղութեանն զարմանային: Եւ բազումք ահաբեկեալք սկսան զրահել պնդապէս, եւ զնոյն շշնջիւն լսէին յամենայն շրթանց:

For even if we were immortal, it would be worthy to die for the love of Christ. For He Himself was immortal, and so loved us, that He took death upon Himself, that by His death we might be saved from eternal death. And since He did not spare His immortality, we too will willfully subject ourselves to death, for love of Him, so that He may willingly receive us in His immortality. We die as mortals, that He may accept our death as that of immortals.

But ask us no more of this, for the covenant of our faith is not with man so that we may stumble like children, but indivisibly with God, from whom we can be neither dissolved nor sundered, not now nor later, nor forever, nor forever and ever.

To this great testament of faith the whole multitude agreed, both great and small; with an honest vow, they swore to remain true to it in life and death.

When this letter arrived at the royal court and was read in the great hall before the whole multitude of the caravan, there were many who rejoiced at the response. Although they cowered in fear from the king, they secretly attested their praise to each other; more so than at its eloquence, they were astonished at its fearlessness. Many of those who were awe-struck began to regain their strength and the same murmurings were heard from all lips.

CHAPTER II

Իսկ չարասէր մոգպետն հանդերձ մեծ հազարապետաւն շնչեաց չարախաւսութիւն, եւ բորբոքեաց զթագաւորն իբրեւ զհուր անշիջանելի: Եւ սկսաւ կրճտել զատամունսն իբրեւ զաւրհասական վիրաւոր. եւ յայտ յանդիման ձայն արձակեաց առ մեծ հրապարակն եւ ասէ.

«Գիտեմ ես զչարութիւն բազմութեան մարդկանս, որ թերահաւատ են ի մերոց աւրինացս, եւ զկնի կախարդութեան մոլորեալ են անդարձութեամբ: Եւ իմ եղեալ է ի մտի, թէ ոչ ումեք թողացուցից ի մեծամեծ հարուածոցն, մինչեւ ակամայ ի բաց կացցեն յայնպիսի վրիպական աւրինաց. եթէ ոք կարի ի մերձաւորաց իցէ, զնոյն անցս եւ ընդ նա անցուցից»:

Յայնժամ ծերն դառնացեալ բանս ի ներքս ընկէց, եւ ասէ ցթագաւորն. «Առ ի՞նչ է քո այդ մեծ տրտմութիւնդ. զի եթէ կայսր չելանէ ըստ քո հրաման, եւ Հոնք կան քեզ ի ծառայութեան, ո՞ր մարդ է յերկրի, եթէ կարող է ընդդէմ դառնալ քում հրամանիդ: Տիրաբար հրաման տուր ի ներքս, եւ ամենայն որ ինչ եւ ասես՝ վաղվաղակի կատարի»:

Եւ անդէն թագաւորն ի ներքս կոչեցեալ զդպրապետն, հրամայէր գրել հրովարտակ. եւ ոչ եւս ըստ սովորութեանն, այլ բանս զայրագինս իբր առ ատելիս եւ անպիտանս, չյիշելով ամենեւին զմեծամեծ վաստակս տիրասէր մարդկանն. այլ միայն կոչոյ հրաման տուեալ յականէ յանուանէ զարս, զոր ինքն ճանաչէր, որոց անուանքն են այս:

The malevolent *mogbed* and the great *hazarbed* [Mihr Narseh] breathed calumny, inflaming the king like an unquenchable fire. Then the king started gnashing his teeth as though mortally wounded and said with a loud voice before the great assembly:

"I know the wickedness of all those men who do not believe in our religion, and who irredeemably err in sorcery. I have determined to spare no one from a great thrashing—not even my friends—until they reluctantly surrender their erroneous religion!"

Then the embittered old man [Mihr Narseh] interposed, and said to the King: "What is your great vexation for? For if the caesar does not abjure your command and the Huns are subject to your dominion, what man on earth can possibly turn against your command? Issue a royal decree, and whatever you say will be accomplished at once."

The king then called in his scribe and commanded him to write an edict; not in the customary style, but with furious words, as though it were addressed to detestable and useless people, without remembering at all the great profits of these men who had been faithful to their master, but summoning name by name those whom he recognized, who were:

Ի տոհմէն Սիւնեաց ՎԱՍԱԿ անուն:
Ի տոհմէն Արծրունեաց ՆԵՐՇԱՊՈՒՀ անուն:
Ի տոհմէն Ռշտունեաց ԱՐՏԱԿ անուն:
Ի տոհմէն Խորխոռունեաց ԳԱԴԵՇՈՅ անուն:
Ի տոհմէն Մամիկոնէից ՎԱՐԴԱՆ անուն:
Ի տոհմէն Մոկաց ԱՐՏԱԿ անուն :
Ի տոհմէն Ապահունեաց ՄԱՆԷՃ անուն:
Ի տոհմէն Ամատունեաց ՎԱՀԱՆ անուն:
Ի տոհմէն Վահեւունեաց ԳԻՒՏ անուն:
Ի տոհմէն Անձեւացեաց ՇՄԱՒՈՆ անուն:

Զայս նախարարքս յականէ յանուանէ կոչեցին ի դուռն արքունի, եւ կէսքն առ նմա իսկ էին ի կարաւանին, եւ այլքն ի կողմանց հիւսիսոյ ի Հոնաց պահակին. թողեալ էր զոմանս ի նախարարացն անդէն յաշխարհին Հայոց:

Արդ թէպէտ եւ ոչ համագունդ ի միոջ վայրի դիպեցան ամենեքեան, սակայն յառաջագոյն գիտացեալ զխորհուրդս չարաբարոյ բռնաւորին, եւ զհեռաւորսն եւս իբրեւ զմերձաւորս ի միոջ վայրի առ միմեանս համարէին:

Եւ ի ձեռն սրբոյն Յովսեփու եպիսկոպոսի նովին ուխտիւ հաստատեալ՝ խաղացին գնացին յիւրաքանչիւր տեղեաց ի դուռն արքունի: Եւ յոյժ փութային վասն եղբարց եւ որդեաց եւ սիրելի դայեկասնունդ բնակացն, որ չարաչար կային ի մեծի նեղութեանն: Վասն որոյ եւ նոքա զանձինս ի մահ մատնեցին՝ ոչ ինչ զանգիտելով իբրեւ զանարի վատասիրտս. այլ յոյժ քաջութեամբ պնդեցին զանձինս, զի թերեւս կարասցեն փրկել զնոսա ի մեծամեծ հարուածոցն:

Of the house of Syunik, Vasak;
Of the house of Artsrunik, Nershapuh;
Of the house of Rshtunik, Artak;
Of the house of Khorkhorunik, Gadesho;
Of the house of the Mamikonians, Vartan;
Of the house of Mokk, Artak;
Of the house of Apahunik, Manech;
Of the house of Amatunik, Vahan;
Of the house of Vahunik, Giwt;
Of the house of Antsevatsik, Shmavon.

These nakharars were summoned name by name to the royal court; half of them were already near the king in the caravan while others were in the northern regions in the pass of the Huns. But he had not summoned some of the nakharars in Armenia.

Now, although they were not all together in one place, they nevertheless recognized in advance the design of the evil despot, and those near and far alike considered themselves to be together in the same place.

Being established in the same covenant under the holy bishop, Hovsep, they went forth, each from his place to the royal court. They made great haste for the sakes of their brothers, sons and dear foster brothers, who were in great trouble. They thus prepared to deliver themselves to death, not as cowards who were faint of heart, but with great virtue they asserted themselves, that they might succeed in rescuing their loved ones from great afflictions.

CHAPTER II

Եւ իբրեւ հասին ի դուռն արքունի, ի մեծի շաբաթու զատկին յանդիման լինէին թագաւորին: Բայց թէպէտ եւ տեսանէին զեղբարս իւրեանց ի մեծամեծ վիշտս տառապանաց, որ վասն անուանն Քրիստոսի ճգնեալք էին պընդապէս, ոչ ինչ տրտում եւ տխուր զերեսս ցուցանէին հրապարակին: Եւ որչափ նոքա զուարթագին երեւէին ամենեցուն, առաւել զարմանային չարաւէրքն:

Եւ զի աւրէնք էին յառաջ ժամանակաւ, յորժամ ի Հայոց այրուձի ի դուռն երթայր ի ձեռն պատուաւորի զաւրագըլխի ուրուք, այր ընդ առաջ յղէր, եւ հարցանէր զողջոյն եւ զխաղաղութիւն Հայոց աշխարհին, եւ երկիցս եւ երիցս անգամ զնոյն առնէր, եւ զհանդէս գնդին ինքնին տեսանէր եւ յառաջ քան ի գործ պատերազմին հասանել զգալն իսկ առ նա՝ մեծ շնորհակալութիւն համարէր, եւ առաջի աթոռակցացն իւրոց եւ ամենայն մեծամեծացն՝ գովութիւն մատուցանէր ամենեցուն, եւ յիշէր զնախնեացն զվաստակս, եւ զառն առն քաջութիւն պատմէր նոցա:

Իսկ այն աւր եւ ոչ մի ինչ յայսցանէ ամենեւին ինչ ոչ յիշեաց. այլ իբրեւ զչարադեւ մի՝ ոչ դադարէր յուզել եւ շարժել զբուք ձմերայնւոյ: Որպէս եւ նմանեալ իսկ էր ծովածուփ ալէկոծ խռովութեան, ոչ դուզնաքեայ վերի վերոյ, այլ անդստին յանդնդոց բարձրանայր փրփրեալ կուտակեալ, վիշապաձայն որոտալով, գազանաբար գոչելով առհասարակ դողացուցանէր զտիեզերական զիւր իշխանութիւնն, որպէս զի փլեալ տարածանից ի համատարած ամենայն ի վերայ լերանց, խորոց, ձորոց՝ ապականել միանգամայն զլայնութիւն դաշտացն վայելչութեան:

It was on the Great Sabbath before Easter that they arrived at the royal court and appeared before the king. Though they saw their brothers, who for the sake of Christ's name were in great danger and misery, they showed neither downcast nor sorrowful faces before the assembly. The more joyous they appeared to everyone, the more the malevolent ones were surprised.

In former times it was customary that when the Armenian cavalry went to the royal court headed by a distinguished general, the king would send a man to greet them, and ask how things fared and about the peace of Armenia, twice and three times, and would inspect the troops himself. He would express great appreciation for their arrival before war and praise them all before his colleagues and all the grandees, recalling the service of their ancestors and relating the valiance of each man.

But on that day, no one remembered this at all; rather, [the king] did not hesitate to unleash a blizzard like an evil demon. He resembled the uproar of a stormy and tempestuous sea that, not merely on the surface, but rising from its depths, foamed, crashed and thundered like the sound of a dragon, shouted like a beast, and filled his entire kingdom with general alarm, as though it would collapse upon all the mountains and valleys, and destroy at once the expanse of the beautiful plains.

Մոնչելով բարբառ արձակեալ եւ ասէ. «Երդուեալ իմ յարեգակն, ի մեծնաստուած, որ ճառագայթիւքն իւրովք լուսաւորէ զամենայն տիեզերս, եւ ջերմութեամբքն կենդանածնէ զամենայն գոյացեալսն, եթէ ոչ վաղիւ ընդ առաւաւտն, ընդ երեւումն սքանչելույն, ընդ իս իւրաքանչիւր ծունր նմա ոչ կրկնեսջիք՝ խոստովանելով զնա աստուած, ոչ ինչ թողացուցից ձեզ՝ զամենայն նեղութիւնս չարչարանացն ի վերայ ածելով, մինչեւ ակամայ կատարիցէք զկամս հրամանաց իմոց»:

Իսկ հաւատացեալքն հաստատեալք ի Քրիստոս՝ ոչ ի սառնամանեաց ձմերայնւոյն հովանային, եւ ոչ ի տապոյ խորշակին ջեռնուին, եւ ոչ յահագին ձայնէն սարսէին, եւ ոչ ի սպառնալեաց տանջանացն զանգիտէին. այլ ի վերհայեցեալք՝ զզաւրութիւնն Քրիստոսի յաւգնութիւն եկեալ տեսանէին, եւ զուարթագին դիմաւք եւ համեստ բանիւք յառաջ մատուցեալ՝ տային պատասխանի թագաւորին.

«Խնդրեմք ի քէն, արքայ քաջ, ունկն դիր սակաւ բանից մերոց, եւ քաղցրութեամբ լուր զոր ասելոցս եմք:

«Քանզի յիշեցուցանեմք քեզ զժամանակն Շապհոյ արքայից արքայի, որ էր հայր հաւուն քո Յազկերտի, եւ ետ նմա Աստուած զերկիրն Հայոց ի ծառայութիւն սովին աւրինաւք, որով եւ մեք իսկ վարիմք այժմ. եւ հարքն մեր եւ հաւք հարցն մերոց կացին նմա ի ծառայութեան վաստակս, եւ սիրով կատարէին զամենայն հրաման բանի նորա, եւ բազում անգամ ի նմանէ մեծապարգեւք լինէին: Եւ յայնց ժամանակաց մինչեւ ի քո հայրենի աթոռդ՝ եւ մեք զնոյն ծառայութիւն ծառայեցաք. բայց թերեւս քեզ լաւագոյն քան զառաջնոցն»:

With a roar he called out and said, "I have sworn by the Sun, the great god, who with its rays shines upon the entire world and by its warmth animates all existence; that if tomorrow morning every knee does not bow before its marvelous appearance and confess it as god, I shall not cease to bring upon you all manner of troubles and suffering, until you conform yourselves, willingly or unwillingly, to the desire of my command."

But the faithful of Christ were not cooled by the icy windstorm, nor scorched by these hot winds, nor shaken by his formidable voice, nor did they turn away from the threat of torture; instead, they looked up and saw that the strength of Christ had come to their help, and with joyful faces and modest words, they answered the king:

"Pray, excellent King, listen to our few words, listen sweetly to what we have to say.

"We remind you of the time of Shapur,[23] king of kings, who was the father of your grandfather Yazdegerd, and to whom God gave Armenia in servitude with the same religion by which we now yet live. Our fathers and great grandfathers obediently served him, and courteously fulfilled all his commands, and were frequently much distinguished by him. And from that time until your accession to the throne of your fathers, we have performed the same service, and perhaps better for you than for your predecessors."

23 Shapur II, 309-379.

CHAPTER II

Զայս ասելով ցուցանէին զքաջութիւն արութեանցն լաւագոյն քան զառաջնոցն ըստ զինուորութեան կարգի: Իսկ զմտից եւ զսակից, եւ որ այլեւս էին հարկ աշխարհին, բազմագոյն քան առ հարբն նորա երթայր յարքունիս: «Նա եւ ի սուրբ եկեղեցւոյն, որ էր ազատ ի Քրիստոս ըստ կարգի նախնեացն մերոց ի սկզբանէ, եւ դու ընդ հարկաւ եդիր. եւ մեք առ սէր քոյոյ տէրութեանդ ոչ ինչ ընդդիմացաք քեզ: Արդ վասն է՞ր յուզեալ իցէ ցասումնս այս ի վերայ մեր. ասա դու մեզ զպատճառս վնասուն. եթէ աւրէ՞նքըն մեր պատճառք իցեն անվաստակ լինելոյ առաջի քո»:

Իսկ չարադեւն լի ամենայն նենգութեամբ՝ զերեսս ի մի կոյս դարձուցեալ եւ ասէ. «Վնաս համարիմ ընդունել ի գանձ արքունի զհարկս աշխարհին ձերոյ, եւ անաւգուտ զքաջութիւն արութեան ձերոյ. քանզի տգիտաբար մոլորեալ էք ի ճշմարիտ աւրինացս մերոց, եւ զաստուածս անարգէք եւ զկրակ սպանանէք եւ զջուրս պղծէք, եւ զմեռեալս ի հող թաղելով զերկիր ապականէք, եւ քրպիկար չառնելով ոյժ տայք Հարամանոյ. եւ որ մեծ քան զամենայն, զի հանապազ ի կանայս ոչ մերձենայք. եւ մեծապէս լինի դիւաց խնդութիւն, չխրատելով ձեր եւ չպահելով զամենայն կարգս մոգաց: Տեսանեմ զձեզ իբրեւ զխաշինս ցրուեալս եւ վայրատեալս յանապատի, եւ յոյժ զեղջ է մտաց իմոց, թէ գուցէ աստուածքն բարկացեալ վասն ձեր՝ ի մէնջ վրէժս առնուցուն: Այլ դուք եթէ կամիք կեալ եւ կեցուցանել զանձինս ձեր եւ մեծարանաւք անդրէն յուղարկիլ, զոր ասացի՝ վաղիւ վաղվաղակի կատարեցէք»:

In saying this, they showed their courage and valor in military rank to be greater than that of their ancestors, and their tributes and dues, combined with all other taxes on the country that flowed into the court, was now greater than in the days of his father. "And you levied taxes upon the holy church, which had liberty in Christ from the beginning according to the arrangement of our ancestors—and we, out of love for your lordship, did not resist you at all. Now, why has this anger been provoked against us? Tell us why we have been accused. Does our religion make us appear unprofitable to you?"

Then that evil demon, full of every guile, turned his face to one side and said: "I consider it a detriment to accept the tributes of your land into the royal treasury, and your valor of no benefit; for you ignorantly err from the truth of our religion and dishonor our god and kill the fire and defile the water, and by burying your dead you corrupt the earth, and by not fulfilling good works, you render assistance to Ahriman. Above all, you do not always approach women, and great is the joy of the demons when you fail to correct your ways and follow all the institutions of the magi. I view you as a flock that is scattered and forsaken in the wilderness and I fear greatly that the gods may become angry because of you and take their revenge upon us. But if you wish to live and save yourselves and be respected again, then do as I said right away.

Յայնժամ երանելի նախարարքն առ հասարակ զձայնըս իւրեանց բարձին եւ ասեն յանդիման ամենեցուն. «Մի՛ դու, արքայ, եւ մի՛ զայդ այլ առ մեզ ասեր. քանզի ոչ է եկեղեցի շինուած մարդոյ, եւ ոչ տուրք արեգական, որպէս դուդ այլ ընդ այլոյ կարծես՝ թէ աստուած իցէ. ոչ միայն զի աստուած չէ, այլ եւ կենդանի չէ: Այլ եկեղեցիք ոչ են պարգեւք թագաւորաց, եւ ոչ արուեստ ճարտարութեանց, եւ ոչ գիւտք իմաստնոց, եւ ոչ աւար քաջութեան զինուորաց, եւ ոչ պատիր խաբէութիւնք դիւաց. նա եւ բնաւ իսկ ամենեւին զինչ եւ ասացես յերկրաւորացս, կամ ի վեհից կամ ի վատթարաց, բնաւ ուրեք եկեղեցի ի նոցանէ ոչ գտցի: Այլ շնորհք են մեծին Աստուծոյ, ոչ միում ումեք ի մարդկանէ տուեալ, այլ ամենայն բանաւոր ազգաց, որք վիճակեալք են ի բնակութիւն ի ներքոյ արեգականս: Հիմունք նորա եդեալ են ի վերայ հաստատուն վիմի. ոչ ներքինք շարժել կարեն. եւ ոչ վերինք դրդուեցուցանել: Եւ զոր երկինք եւ երկիր ոչ դողացուցանէ, մի՛ ոք ի մարդկանէ խրոխտացի յաղթել նմա: Հա՛պա, որով աւրինակաւ զինչ կամիս առնել, կատարեա. պատրաստ եմք ամենեքեան առ ամենայն մեքենայս հարուածոցն տանջանաց, զոր սպառնացար. ոչ միայն ի չարչարել, այլ եւ ի մեռանել: Եւ եթէ դարձեալեւս զնոյն բանս հարցանես, ի միոջէ միոջէ լուիցես առաւել քան զդոյն պատասխանի»:

Յայնժամ դառնացեալ քան զլեղի թագաւորն՝ փլուզանէր անդէն իփորին զծով կամաւոր մաղձոյն իւրոյ. եւ ընդ քիթսն եւ ընդ բերանն առ հասարակզոլոշի ջերմախառն ելանէր, իբրեւ ի սաստիկ հնոցէ ծուխ թանձրացեալ:

Then the venerable nakharars raised their voices in one accord and said before everyone: "Speak no more, king! For the church is not made by men, nor given by the sun, which you and others take for a god. Not only is the sun not a god, it is not even animate. And churches are not gifts of kings, nor are they constructed by skill, nor are they discoveries of wise men, nor the spoil of valiant armies, nor the deception of demons. Whatever you have to say of us worldly beings, whether grand or ill, none of us have ever founded a church. Churches are a blessing from the great God, which He has not granted to one man, but to all rational nations who were made to live under the sun. Its foundation is established on firm stone, which neither those above nor those below can move. And that which heaven and earth cannot shake, let no man boast of conquering. Do therefore as you wish; we are prepared for all machinations of torments and sufferings with which you threaten us—and not only torture, but also death. Now should you repeat the same question, so often will you hear more of the same from each of us."

Then the king, turning more bitter than gall, poured forth the sea of bile from his stomach and warm vapor emanated from his nose and mouth, like thick smoke from a furnace.

Եւ առ չհանդուրժել սրտին իւրոյ՝ կոտորէր զզաւրութիւն մարմնոյն, եւ ծակոտէր զբազմամթեր աման խորհրդոցն, ցրուէր եւ վատնէր զամենայն խորհուրդն նենգութեան: Եւ զոր ոչ երբէք կամէր իւրոց սիրելեացն յայտնել, ակամայ առաջի ծառայիցն Քրիստոսի մերկանայր եւ դնէր զամենայն կարգաւ:

Երեքկնէր եւ չորեքկնէր զանսուտ երդումն յարեգակն, եւ ասէր այսպէս. «Ոչ կարէք աւերել զանխաբ ամուրս իմ. եւ ոչ որում ցանկացեալդ էք՝ վաղվաղակի տամ գտանել ձեզ. այլ զամենեսեան զձեզ եւ որ ի գնդիս են՝ չարաչար կապանաւք ի Սագաստան տամ անցուցանել ընդ անճանապարհ տեղիս, որ եւ բազումք ի ձէնջ ի խորշակէ յերթալն սատակիցին, եւ մնացեալքն անկցին ի բերդս ամուրս եւ ի բանդս անելս: Եւ ի ձեր աշխարհին առաքեցից զաւրս անթիւ հանդերձ փղաւք, եւ զկին եւ զորդիս ի Խուժաստան տամ խաղացուցանել. եւ զեկեղեցիս եւ զոր անուանէք վկայարանս՝ քակեցից, քանդեցից եւ յապականութիւն դարձուցից. եւ եթէ ոք ընդդէմ դարձեալ գտցի, կոխանեղեալ գազանաց՝ անողորմ մեռանիցի: Եւ զամենայն ասացեալս արարից եւ կատարեցից առ մնացորդս աշխարհին»:

Եւ վաղվաղակի հրամայէր զպատուական նախարարսն հանել մեծաւ անարգանաւք յերեսաց իւրոց. եւ զգուշութեամբ հրաման տուեալ դահճապետին՝ առանց կապանաց յիւրաքանչիւր վանս պահել, եւ ինքն զառածեալ անդրէն դառնայր անմխիթար տրտմութեամբ զաւթեւանս ագանէր:

His heart could not bear it and the strength of his body was zapped, piercing the brimming vessel of his deceitful plans, scattering and dissipating them all. And that which he did not resolve to reveal even to his friends, he involuntarily revealed in detail before the servants of Christ.

Three or four times he swore an undisguised oath to the sun, and said [to the Christians]: "You cannot ruin my inviolable fortresses, nor will I allow you to acquire that which you desire so easily. But I will take all of you together with those who are in my army with crushing chains to Sagastan through impassable places, where the greater part of you will die on the way from the heat, and the remainder will be thrown into a strong fortress and inescapable prison. I will send into your country an innumerable force with many elephants. Your wives and children will be driven to Khuzestan, and your churches and what you call martyria I shall demolish, destroy and ruin. Should anyone resist, he will be trampled by wild beasts and die a merciless death, and I will gather and effect all this upon those who remain in your land."

Then he immediately ordered the distinguished nakharars to be led away from his sight in shame, and carefully commanded the captain of the guard to lodge each of them separately, unbound, and he himself returned again to inconsolable despair in his quarters.

CHAPTER II

Իսկ հաւատացեալքն ճշմարտութեամբ ի Քրիստոս՝ ոչ ինչ երկմտութեամբ թերահաւատէին յառաջին խրատուէ սուրբ վարդապետացն իւրեանց. այլ տակաւին ի խնդիր էին հնարիցն, թէ ո՛րպէս զանձինս եւ զսիրելիս հանցեն ի մեծ նեղութենէն: Եւ բազում անգամ ջանալով, եւ մեծամեծացն՝ որ աւգնականք էին նոցա ի Դրանն արքունի՝ խոստմունս մեծամեծս առաջի դնէին նոցա առ ի այս կարաւոյ, եւ ոչ սակաւ զանձս առժամայն ծախէին նոցա:

Եւ իբրեւ յամենայն կողմանց եկն փակեցաւ անել արգելան նոցա, յայնժամ զխորհուրդն Աբրահամու ի մէջ առեալ՝ աղաղակէին եւ ասէին ի սիրտս իւրեանց. «Ամենեցուն մեր նուիրեալ եւ եղեալ զեղբարս եւ զորդիս եւ զամենայն սիրելիս ընդ կապանաւք իբրեւ զԻսահակ ի վերայ սուրբ սեղանոյն, ընկալ, Տէր, զկամաւոր պատարագս մեր, եւ մի՛ տար զեկեղեցի քո յայպն կատականաց անաւրէն իշխանիս այսորիկ»:

Մի ոմն ի ներքին խորհրդակցացն արքայի ի ծածուկ ունէր զանքակ սէրն ի Քրիստոս, քանզի մկրտեալ իսկ էր յաւազանն կենդանի, եւ մեծապէս հոգտանէր հնարից կենաց վշտացելոցն: Եւ իբրեւ ստուգեաց ճշմարտիւ, եթէ զոր սպառնացաւ թագաւորն զամենայն չարիսն՝ կամի անցուցանել ընդ աշխարհին Հայոց, թէպէտ եւ ոչ ամենեցուն՝ այլ սակաւուց ի նոցանէ ուսոյց զխրատ հնարից՝ զի առ անգամ մի ի նեղութենէ անտի զանձինս ապրեցուսցեն:

But the true believers in Christ did not at all draw back and doubt the initial advice of their holy vardapets; yet still they were devising means to remove themselves and their friends from this great trouble. And trying many times, the grandees who had helped them in the royal court were enticed with great promises and bought off with no small amount of riches.

When their ineluctable prison was locked on all sides, the thought of Abraham occurred to them and they cried and said in their hearts: "We have all offered our brothers and sons and all our loved ones, bound like Isaac on the holy altar. Receive, O Lord, our voluntary oblation, and do not deliver your Church to the ridicule and mockery of this depraved ruler."

One of the king's advisors secretly had an indestructible love of Christ, for he had been baptized in the font of life, and took great care to save the lives of those who were afflicted. And when he confirmed that the king threatened to take out all his malice upon Armenia, he advised some of them about the means by which to extricate themselves from their trouble for a while.

CHAPTER II

Եւ մինչդեռ գունդ կազմէին, որ զնոսա շկաւթակ առաջեն յանդարձ աւտարութիւն, որպէս զբազում նախարարսն ի Վրաց աշխարհէն արարին, ի նմին ժամանակի գուժկան հասանէր ի կողմանցն Քուշանաց, եթէ գունդ հատաւ ի թշնամեացն, որ ելին աւերեցին զգաւառս բազումս արքունի: Եւ այս լինէր մեծ աւգնականութիւն նոցա յերկնից: Եւ անաւրէնն ճեպեալ տագնապէր զայրուձին յառաջ արձակել, եւ ինքն փութով ստէպ զհետ երթայր. եւ ի խոր խոցեալ զխորհուրդսն՝ ցրուէր զառաջին հաստատուն երդումն:

Իսկ երկիւղածացն Տեառն զայս տեսեալ՝ մեծաւ յուսով աղաւթս առնէին եւ ասէին միաբան. «Դու Տէ՛ր ամենայնի, որ գիտես զծածկեալս սրտից մարդկան, եւ յայտնի են առաջի քո ամենայն աներեւոյթք խորհրդոց, եւ ոչ ինչ խնդրես վկայութիւն յերեւելեացս, որպէս զի եւ զանգործս մեր տեսանեն աչք քո, արդ առաջի քո հեղումք զխընդրրուածս մեր: Ընկալ, Տէր, զծածկութիւն աղաւթից մերոց, եւ կատարեա զմեզ ի հաճոյս պատուիրանաց քոց, զի ամաչեսցէ չարն, որ խրոխտացեալ մարտնչի մեզ իշխանութեամբ անաւրինին: Շարժեա, Տէր, զկամակոր խորհուրդս նենգաւորին, եւ խափանեցո զկամս ամբարշտութեան նորա, եւ դարձո զմեզ խաղաղական խորհրդով անդրէն ի սուրբ եկեղեցին. զի մի՛ յանկարծակի յափշտակեալ աւերեսցի չարաչար ի թշնամեաց»:

And while they were gathering an army to send them into exile without return, as they had done with many nakharars in Iberia, a messenger arrived from the land of the Kushans bearing unhappy news, that a detachment of the enemy had broken loose and destroyed many royal districts. This turned out to be a great boon for the Armenians from heaven, for in a panic the abominable king hastily sent forth his cavalry, and himself diligently followed them. His plans being foiled, he broke his firm oath.

When those who feared the Lord saw this, they became filled with hope, and said in prayer all together: "O Lord of all, Who knows what lies hidden in the hearts of men, and before Whom all invisible thoughts are evident, Who demand no testimony to that which is perceptible, for Your eyes see that which is latent, now before you we pour forth our prayers! Receive, Lord, our secret prayers, and make us take favor in your commandments, and humble the evil one, who arrogantly combats us with his depraved rule. Shake, Lord, the crooked plan of the deceiver, encumber his impious will, and lead us with peaceful thoughts back to the holy Church, that it not be suddenly attacked and ruined by the wicked enemy."

CHAPTER II

Եւ անձամբք իւրեանց զայս ուխտ եդեալ անքակու-թեամբ ընդ Աստուծոյ, զի հաստատուն կացցեն ըստ առա-ջին խորհրդոցն, պատգամ ի ներքս յղէին զնոյն խրատ-տուն իւրեանց, իբր թէ կատարեսցին կամք անայրէնու-թեան նորա:

Զայն իբրեւ լուաւ թագաւորն՝ յոյժ ցնծացեալ բերկրե-ցաւ, կարծեցեալ զդիսն հասանել նմա յաւգնականութիւն, շրջեալ եւ աւերեալ զհաստատուն խորհուրդս ծառայիցն Աստուծոյ. եւ ահա մատուցաննեն երկրպագութիւն արե-գական, պատուեալ զնա զոհիւք եւ ամենայն աւրինաւք մո-գութեանն:

Եւ զայն ոչ կարաց իմանալ ցնորեալն, եթէ անստուեր լոյսն արեգականն արդարութեան սպառէր եւ մաշէր զխա-ւարային խորհուրդս նորա, եւ եղծեալ ապականէին զամե-նայն խեղաթիւր կամս նորա: Եւ կուրացեալ ի ճշմարիտ յայտնութենէն՝ ոչ ինչ իմացաւ զպատրանս խաբէութեանն, որով վրիպեացն: Հեղոյր արկանէր առաջի նոցա զպար-գեւս երկրաւորս, եւ վերստին ամենեցուն զպատիւս եւ զգահս նորոգէր, յառաջ մատուցանելով եւ երեւելի առնե-լով ընդ ամենայն տիեզերական իշխանութիւնն: Եւ անբաւ առատութեամբ ագարակս եւ աւանս միում միում նոցա յարքունուստ շնորհէր. սիրելիս եւ բարեկամս կարդայր զնոսա, եւ առ հպարտ յանդգնութեան մտացն կամակո-րութեան՝ կարծէր եթէ փոխանակիցի ճշմարտութիւնն ընդ ստութեան:

Having made this vow of indissolubility with God to remain firm in their former resolve, they sent a message with their same advisor pretending that they would conform to the king's impious will.

When the king heard this, he rejoiced exceedingly, supposing that the gods had arrived to assist him, and had overturned and destroyed the firm resolution of the servants of God; and behold, they offered to worship the sun, honoring it with offerings and all the customs of the magi.

But the deranged one could not understand that the undimmed light of the Sun of Righteousness was consuming his dark intentions and corrupting his depraved will. Blinded by the true revelation, he did not at all understand the deceitful trickery with which they caused him to err. He poured out before them earthly gifts and renewed their honors and distinctions, elevating them and distinguishing them throughout his worldly dominion. And to each of them he bestowed an immense abundance of farms and villages from the royal land; he called them dear friends, and in the rashness of his perverse mind, he thought that truth could be exchanged for a lie.

Եւ զայս արարեալ, բազում այրուձի գումարէր ընդ նոսա, եւ ի մոգուցն ոչ սակաւս, աւելի քան զեւթն հարիւր վարդապետս յղէր ընդ նոսա, եւ զմեծ ոմն իշխան մոգպետ կացուցանէր ի վերայ նոցա: Խոնարհէր եւ աղաչէր պատուիրելով, թէ մինչ ես ի պատերազմէս դարձեալ գայցեմ խաղաղութեամբ, ձեր արարեալ եւ կատարեալ իցէ զամենայն ըստ կամաց իմոց: Եւ այսպէս շքով եւ պատուով առաջնորդէր նոցա զերկայնութիւն ճանապարհին անդրէն յերկիրն Հայոց: Եւ ինքն աւետիս խնդալիս առաքէր յատրուշանս բազումս, գրէր եւ ցուցանէր մոգաց եւ մոգպետաց եւ ամենայն մեծամեծաց կողմանց կողմանց աշխարհաց՝ ո՛րպէս դիցն աւգնականութեամբ զգործ քաջութեան իմոյ յառաջ մատուցեալ:

Իսկ խոհերականքն այնուհետեւ յարուցեալ յիւրաքանչիւր խաւարային դարանաց՝ իղձք լինէին վաղվաղակի զհրամանն կատարել. ձայն արարեալ յաշխարհս հեռաւորս՝ միանգամայն խաղալ գնալ յերկիրն արեւմտից: Եւ մինչ չեւ հասեալ էին ի մեծ աշխարհն Հայոց, փայտ ընկենուին եւ վիճակս արկանէին, թէ ո՛ր լեզու որո՛մ դասու հասցէ յաշակերտութիւն: Զի առհասարակ հրաման առեալ էր յարքունուստ, որպէս Հայոց աշխարհին, նոյնպէս եւ Վրաց եւ Աղուանից եւ Լփնաց, Աղձնեաց եւ Կորդուաց եւ Ծաւդէից եւ Դասն եւ որ այլ եւս ուրեք ուրեք ի ծածուկ յիշխանութեանն Պարսից ունէին զքրիստոնէութիւն:

Having done this, he assembled a large cavalry unit for them, and many magi, and sent more than 700 teachers with them, and appointed over them a great prince as mogbed. Humbly and pleadingly, he ordered, "You shall have carried out everything according to my will by the time I return in peace from this war." With honor and esteem he sent them on their journey to Armenia, sent joyful tidings to many fire temples, and wrote and announced to all the magi, mogbeds, and all the magnates in all quarters of the land that he had accomplished his valiant work with the help of the gods."

The unclean ones then broke from their dark ambushes, eager to quickly fulfill the king's command. They called out to distant lands, to go at once into the land of the West, and before they had reached the land of Greater Armenia, they threw wood to cast lots to decide on who would instruct the students. For they had taken general orders from the royal court to instruct not only the land of Armenia, but also Georgia, Aghuank, Lpink, Aghdznik, Korduk, Tsodik, Dasn, and all those who secretly followed Christianity in the dominion of the Persians.

CHAPTER II

Եւ անզգայ յարձակմամբ յաւարի առնուլ փութային զգանձս սուրբ եկեղեցեացն, եւ իբրեւ զդեւս այնուհետեւ միմեանց պատահէին: Եւ լինէր գունդ զաւրաց բազմաց, եւ չարասէրն սատանայ իբրեւ զաւրավար ի մէջ նոցա երեւէր, եւ անդադար յորդորելով զամենեսեան ճեպեալ փութացուցանէր: Կէտ եղեալ զժամանակն՝ զամիսն վեցերորդ, տագնապէին եւ ստիպէին արքունի հրամանաւ:

«Մինչեւ ի նաւասարդէ ի նաւասարդ, աւէ, յամենայն տեղիս՝ որ իցեն ընդ իշխանութեամբ թագաւորին մեծի, բարձցին կարգք եկեղեցւոյ, փակեսցին եւ կնքեսցին դրբունք սուրբ տաճարացն, գրով համարով առցին նուիրեալ սպասքն յարքունիս, լռեսցեն ձայնք սաղմոսացն եւ դադարեսցեն ընթերցուածք անսուտ մարգարէիցն: Քահանայք մի՛ իշխեսցեն ի տունս իւրեանց ուսուցանել զժողովուրդս, եւ հաւատացեալքն ի Քրիստոս՝ արք եւ կանայք, որ բնակեալ են յիւրաքանչիւր մենանոցս, փոխեսցեն զհանդերձս իւրեանց ըստ աշխարհական կարգաց:

Դարձեալ եւ կանայք նախարարացն կալցին զուսումն վարդապետութեան մոգացն: Ուստերք եւ դստերք ազատաց եւ շինականաց կրթեսցին ի հրահանգս նոցուն մոգաց: Կարճեսցին եւ արգելցին աւրէնք սուրբ ամուսնութեան, զոր ունէին ի նախնեաց ըստ կարգի քրիստոնէութեանն. այլ փոխանակ ընդ կնոջ միոյ՝ բազում կանայս արասցեն. զի աճեցեալ բազմասցին ազգք Հայոց: Դստերք հարանց լինիցին, եւ քորք՝ եղբարց. մարք մի՛ ելցեն յորդւոց, այլ եւ թոռունք ելցեն յանկողինս հաւուց:

And with a senseless attack they hurriedly robbed the treasures of the holy churches and gathered together like demons, forming a great force. The malicious Satan appeared among them like a general, incessantly inciting them all to hurry. They strained and hastened to execute the royal ordinance by the sixth month.

"From Navasard to Navasard",[24] he said, "in all places that are in the dominion of the great king, the services of the Church shall be stopped, the doors of the holy temples closed and sealed, the holy vessels accounted for and taken to the royal court, the singing of the psalms silenced, and the reading of the true prophets discontinued. The priests shall not be at liberty to teach people in their houses, and the believers of Christ who dwell in their own hermitages shall be forced to exchange their clothing to the worldly type, both men and women alike.

"Similarly, the nakharars' wives must accept the teaching and doctrine of the magi. The sons and daughters of the azats and peasants shall be educated by the instruction of the same magi. They shall cancel and abolish the customs of holy matrimony, which they had from their forefathers according to Christian rites; and instead of one wife they shall take many, to increase and multiply the Armenian people. The daughters shall be wives for their fathers, and the sisters for their brothers; but mothers not for sons, although grandchildren shall ascend the couch with their grandparents.[25]

24 The first month of the Armenian year.
25 Part of the Zoroastrian custom of 'xwedodah' (conosanguine marriage).

Պատրուճակք մի՛ մեռցին անյազ, եթէ յաւդեաց իցէ եւ եթէ յայծեաց եւ եթէ յարջառոց եւ եթէ ի հաւուց եւ եթէ ի խոզաց: Հայսք առանց փանդամի մի՛ զանգցին. ծիւք եւ քակորք ի կրակ մի՛ եկեսցեն. ձեռք առանց գումիզոյ մի՛ լուասցին. շնջրիք եւ աղուէսք եւ նապաստակք մի՛ մեռցին: Աւձք եւ մողէսք, գորտք եւ մրջմունք, եւ որ այլ եւս խառնափնդոր բազմաճճիք են, մի՛ կայցեն, այլ վաղ թուով համարով ի մէջ բերցեն ըստ արքունի չափոյն: Եւ որ այլ եւս ինչ սպասք իցեն, կամ զոհից կամ սպանդից, ըստ տաւնական կարգին՝ տարեւորթուականին, եւ ըստ կապճաթիւ մոխրաչափ կարգին:

Զայս ամենայն զոր ասացաք՝ առ ժամանակ մի մինչեւ ի գլուխ տարւոյ կատարեսցեն ամենեքեան. եւ զայլն ամենայն առ յապա պատրաստեսցեն»:

Իսկ զայս ամենայն հրաման պատուիրանաց առեալ մոգաց եւ մոգպետաց, զտիւ եւ զգիշեր փութային հասանել յաշխարհին Հայոց. եւ առ յոյժ խնդութեանն ոչ երբէք յագէին երկայնութեամբ ճանապարհին:

"Sacrificial animals should not be slaughtered without being offered to the gods, whether they be sheep, goats, cattle, fowl, or pigs. Dough shall not be kneaded without a veil; excrements and dung shall not be thrown into the fire; hands shall not be washed without bull's urine;[26] beavers,[27] foxes and hares shall not be killed. Snakes, lizards, frogs, ants, and various other kinds of worms shall not be left to stand, but immediately accounted for and collected according to the royal order. And what further services there be, either of sacrificial offerings or slaughters, shall be performed according to the yearly calendar of festivals and measure of ashes due.

"All this shall be carried out by everyone until the end of the year; and all else they shall prepare later."

When the magi and mogbeds received all these orders, day and night they hastened to reach Armenia, and from their great joy, they did not at all tire from the length of their journey.

26 Bovine urine ('gōmēz') disinfection, a Zoroastrian purification rite.
27 or, otters.

Գ

ՎԱՍՆ ՄԻԱԲԱՆՈՒԹԵԱՆ ՍՈՒՐԲ ՈՒԽՏԻՆ ԵԿԵՂԵՑԻՈՅ

Թէպէտ եւ ոչ իցեմք բաւական ասել զամենայն չարիսն, որ անցք անցին անդէն ի կարաւանին ընդ գունդն Հայոց, սակայն եւ ոչ լռել կամիմք՝ ծածկելով զվիշտս նեղութեանն. այլ ասասցուք փոքր ի շատէ, զի ձայնակիցք լիցուք այնոցիկ, որք դառնապէս զմեզ ողբային. զի եւ դու իբրեւ լըւիցես՝ ոչ սակաւ արտասուս հեղուցուս ի վերայ ազգիս թըշուառութեան:

Զի ահա անդէն ի մեծ բանակին Պարսից՝ յազգաց ազգաց որք էին հաւատացեալ ի սուրբ աւետարանն Քրիստոսի, իբրեւ տեսին զչար յանձնառութիւնն Հայոց, յոյժ հարան ի միտս իւրեանց, եւ կործանեցան անկան ի վերայ դիմաց իւրեանց: Բազումք ի նոցանէ թաղծեալ ի սուգ ծանրութեան, հարեալ յոգիս եւ դառնացեալ յարտասուս, եկին եւ յանդիմանեցին զնախարարեանն, եւ յոյժ դսրովե-ցին զուխտ քահանայութեանն:

Զզուէին զամենեսեան եւ ասէին. «Զի՞ առնիցէք զսուրբ կտակարանսդ, եւ կամ յո՞ տանիցիք զպաս տէրունեան սեղանոյն. մոռանայցէ՞ք արդեւք զհոգեւոր աւրհնութիւնսդ, եւ կամ լռեալ դադարիցէ՞ք ի մարգարէական ձայնիցդ: Կափուցէք զաչս յընթերցուածոց, եւ խցէք զականջս ի լսելոյ. միթէ զմտացդանմոռացութիւն ո՞չ յիշիցէք: Զի՞նչ առնիցէք զպատուիրեալսն ի Տեառնէ. Որ ուրասցի զիս առաջի մարդկան, յուրացայց եւ ես զնմանէ առաջի Հաւր իմոյ, որ յերկինս է, եւ հրեշտակաց սրբոց:

III

ON THE BROTHERHOOD OF THE FAITHFUL OF THE CHURCH

Although we cannot say enough about all the evils that befell the Armenian regiment there in the caravan, we also do not wish to stay silent and gloss over their great afflictions. Thus, we will narrate what happened in part, that we concord with those who bitterly mourned us and so that when you hear this, you too will shed not a few tears over the misery of our nation.

For behold, in the great encampment of the Persians, the members of the faithful in the Holy Gospel of Christ were struck with fear and fell on their faces when they saw the evil that was visited upon the Armenians. Many of them, their souls stricken, and heavily grieving with bitter tears, came and censured the nakharars and vituperated the clergy.

Cursing them all, they said: "What will you do with your Holy Testaments, or where will you take the vessels of the Lord's altar? Will you forget your spiritual blessings? Will you silence and discontinue the voices of the prophets? Shut your eyes to reading and close your ears to hearing if you will, but have you forgotten about the Lord's command: 'Whoever denies me before men, I also will deny before my Father who is in heaven, and before the holy angels'?[28]

28 Matthew 10:33; Luke 12:9.

«Վարդապետք էիք առաքելական քարոզութեանն. արդ աշակե՞րտք լինիցիք մոլար խաբէութեանն: Ուսուցիչք էիք ճշմարտութեանն, արդ ուսուցանիցէ՞ք զպատիր խաբէութիւն մոգաց: Քարոզք էիք արարչական զաւրութեանն, արդ զտարերս աստուա՞ծս խոստովանիք: Յանդիմանիչք էիք ստութեան, արդ եւ քան զսուտն ստագո՞յնք լինիցիք: Ի հուր եւ ի հոգի էիք մկրտեալք, արդ ի մոխիր եւ յաճի՞ւն թաթաւիցիք. կենդանի մարմնով եւ անմահ արեամբ էիք սնեալ, արդ ի ճենճե՞ր զոհից եւ ի շարաւ աղտեղի՞ս մրճոտիցիք: Տաճար էիք Հոգւոյն Սրբոյ, արդ զոհարան դիւա՞ց լինիցիք. քրիստոսազգեացք էիք ի մանկութենէ, արդ մերկացեալք ի փառացն՝ դիւաբար արեգակա՞ն կաքաւիցէք:

«Ժառանգք էիք արքայութեանն, արդ անձամբ զանձինըս արարէք ժառանգ գեհենին: Նոցա՛ է պատրաստեալ հուրն անշէջ, ընդէ՞ր դուք ընդ նոսա այրեցեալ տոչորեցայք. նոցա՛ պարարի որդն անմահ, իսկ արդ դուք պար արիցէք զմարմինս ձեր նմա ի կերակուր. խաւարն արտաքին նոցա՛ թանձրացեալ պահի, դուք լուսազգեստք՝ ընդէ՞ր յուղարկեցայք ընդ նոսա ի նոյն խաւար: Նոքա ի վաղնջուց հետէ էին իսկ կուրացեալք, դուք զիա՞րդ զկնի կուրացն կուրացարուք: Նոցա՛ էր փորեալ զխորխորատն, դուք ընդէ՞ր լցէք յառաջագոյն: Ե՞րբ ուսանիցիք զբազմաթիւ անուանս աստուածոցն նոցա, այն որ չիք ուրեք ի միջի եւ ոչ մի: Թեթեւացեալք ի ծանր բեռանց՝ անձամբ անձին առէք զբեռն ծանրութեան. ազատեալք ի ծառայութենէ՝ չարաչար մտէք յանազատելի ծառայութիւնն:

"You were teachers of the apostolic preaching; will you now be students of errant deception? You were teachers of truth; will you now teach the enticing trickery of the magi? You were preachers of the power of the Creator; do you now attest the elements as gods? You were admonishers of falsehood; will you now become more bogus than lies? You were baptized with fire and spirit; will you now be immersed in ashes and dust? You were nourished with living flesh and immortal blood; will you now be burnt and blackened from the smoke of immolation and impure pus? You were temples of the Holy Spirit; will you now become sacrificial altars for demons? You had put on Christ since youth; will you now strip yourself of that glory and dance like demons before the sun?

"You were heirs of the kingdom; you have now become heirs of hell. It is they whom the inextinguishable fire has threatened; why then are you burnt and scorched? It is for them that the immortal worm is fattened, yet it is ye who now fatten your bodies to feed them?[29] It is for them that the darkness outside is impenetrable; you, radiant ones, why do you go forth into the same darkness with them? They have long been blind; why then do you follow the blind into blindness? They dug the ditch; why did you fill it first? When will you come to learn the many names of their gods, not one of whom exists anywhere? Relieved of your heavy burden, you yourselves took on the burden of servitude; then, liberated from servitude, you torturously went back into ineluctable slavery.

29 Sirach 7:17.

«Եթէ գիտէիք եւ երեւէր ձեզ յայտնի, սուգ առին երկինք ի վերայ ձեր, եւ թաղծեցաւ երկիրս ի ներքոյ ոտից ձերոց: Հրեշտակք ի վերուստ են ձեզ բարկացեալք, եւ ի յերկրէս մարտիրոսքն են ձեզ ցասուցեալք: Ողորմի՜մ, ողորմիմ սիրելեաց ձերոց, եւ բազում անգամ ողորմիմ անձանց ձերոց: Ջի թէ մարդոյ փրկեալ էր զձեզ ի ծառայութենէ, եւ դուք անձամբ զանձինս այլում ի ծառայութիւն արկանէիք, ի մեծ բարկութիւն բրդէիք զառաջին տէրն ձեր. իսկ արդ զի՞նչ առնիցէք զաստուածաստաստ հրամանն. Ես եմ Աստուած, եւ չիք այլ որ բաց յինէն, եւ ոչ զկնի իմ այլ որ լիցի Աստուած. Աստուած նախանձոտ եմ ես, հատուցանեմ զմեղս հարց յորդիս մինչեւ յեւթն դար: Իսկ եթէ որդիքն արդարք՝ վասն հարցն մեղաց ընդունին զատտակումն, յորժամ ինքեանք որդիքն իսկ մեղիցեն, ո՞չ ահա միանգամայն զանձանց եւ զհարց տայցեն ի միասին:

«Դո՛ւք էիք մեր ամուր պարիսպ ապաստանի. յորժամ աստի վտանգ հասանէր, առ ձեզ յանդորր ելանէաք. արդ մեծ ամուրդ այդ հիմն ի վեր տապալեցաւ: Դո՛ւք էիք մեր պարծանս առ թշնամիսն ճշմարտութեան, արդ դուք էք մեր նախատինք առ նոյն թշնամիս: Յայժմ վասն ձերոյ ճշմարիտ հաւատոցն եւ ի մեզ փոքր ի շատէ խնայէին. եւ արդ ի պատճառս ձեր եւ զմեզ անողորմ դատին: Ոչ միայն զանձանց դատաստան տալոց էք առաջի ահեղ ատենին Աստուծոյ, այլ եւ բազմաց ամենեցուն՝ որ ի ձեր պատճառս եւ զնոսա եւս չարչարեսցեն»:

"If only you knew, if only it was evident to you, that the heavens mourned over you and that the earth sorrowed beneath your feet. The angels above are angry with you, and the earth's martyrs are furious with you. Pity! I pity your loved ones, and much more, I pity you. For if a man had rescued you from servitude, and then you had enslaved yourselves to another master, you would greatly anger your first master. And now what will you do about the wrathful command of God, 'I am God, and aside from me there is none other, and apart from me there will be no other; I am a zealous God, and I shall recompense the iniquity of fathers onto their sons for seven ages.'?[30] Now if the righteous sons accept death for the sins of their fathers, then when the sons themselves sin, will they not at once answer for both themselves and their fathers?

"You were the strong walls of our refuge: when danger loomed, we came to you for safety; now that great stronghold has been destroyed. You were our boast against the enemies of truth, but now you are a cause of reproach before the same enemies. Until now, for the sake of your true faith they partly spared us, and now because of you they pitilessly judge us. Not only will you answer for yourselves before the fearsome tribunal of God, but also for many others whom they shall afflict because of you."

30 Jeremiah, 32:18.

CHAPTER III

Զայս եւ առաւել քան զսոյն խաւսեցան ընդ մեծամեծս աւագանւոյն, եւ յաւելին ցաւս ի վերայ ցաւոց: Յայտնել եւ ցուցանել նոցա զխորհուրդն ոչ կարէին, լռել եւ չառնել պատասխանի անհնար էր. հեղձամղձուկ եղեալ մեծապէս յարտաասուս հարկանէին: Ընդ նոսին դառնացեալ լսողք եւ տեսողք յանմխիթար սուգ լինէին ամենեքեան:

Յայնմ ժամանակի քահանայքն որ անդէն ի զաւրուն էին, առ չժուժալ սրտիցն բարկութեան՝ քակեալ որոշեցան ի նախարարացն եւ յամենայն բազմութենէն. եւ զմի ոմն դեսպան ձիով փութապէս առաքեցին յաշխարհն Հայոց: Գոյժ ի բերան առեալ եւ զաւձիս պատառեալ, հասեալ ի ժողովս եպիսկոպոսացն, մեծապէս յարտասուս հարեալ, կայր եւ պատմէր զամենայնանցս չարչարանացն. այլ ոչ յայտնէր նոցա զծածկութիւն խորհրդոցն:

Յայնմ ժամանակի սփռեցան եպիսկոպոսքն յիւրաքանչիւր իշխանութիւնս, եւ առաքեցին զքորեպիսկոպոսս ի գեաւղս եւ յագարակս եւ ի բազում ամուրս լեռնային գաւառացն: Դրդեցին ժողովեցին զբազմութիւն արանց եւ կանանց, շինականաց եւ ազատաց, զքահանայից եւ զմենակեցաց. խրատ եդին, պնդեցին եւ արարին զամենեսեան զինուորս Քրիստոսի:

Եւ յառաջին բան խորհրդին այս հաստատեցաւ. «Ձեռն եղբաւր հարազատի ի մերձաւոր իւր լիցի, որ անցեալ իցէ ըստ ուխտ պատուիրանին Աստուծոյ. եւ մի՛ խնայեսցէ հայր յորդի, եւ մի՛ ակն առնուցու որդի հաւր պատուոյն:

This, and more than this, they spoke against the grandee nobles, and added pain upon pain. [The nobles] could not reveal their intention, but to remain silent and not respond was also impossible. They choked and burst into great tears. Those who heard and saw became embittered with them, and they all wept inconsolably.

Then the priests, who were in the army and who could no longer endure their hearts' anger, decided to separate themselves from the nakharars and the entire multitude and swiftly sent a messenger by horseback to Armenia. Taking the bad news with him, and with his clothes torn, he reached the assembly of the bishops, burst into copious tears, stood before them and recounted all the tortures that had occurred, but did not reveal to them his secret intentions.

Then the bishops disbanded each to his own diocese, sent the chorbishops to the villages and estates and to the many strongholds of the mountainous districts. They urged an assembly of all the men and women, peasants and nobles, priests and monks. They advised and strengthened them, and rendered them all soldiers of Christ.

The first thing the assembly established was this: "Let the hand of the blood-brother rise against his neighbor who should transgress the covenant of God's commandment—and let father spare not son, nor let son accept a father's honor.[31]

31 Matthew 10:21.

Կին կռուեցի ընդ առն ամուսնոյ, եւ ծառայ դարձցի ընդ-դէմ տեառն իւրոյ։ Աւրէնք աստուածայինք կացցեն թագա-ւոր ի վերայ ամենայնի, եւ ի նմին աւրինաց ընկալցին յան-ցաւորք զպատիժս դատապարտութեան»։

Եւ իբրեւ այս այսպէս հաստատեցաւ կազմեցաւ, երե-ւեցան ամենեքեան զինեալք եւ սաղաւարտեալք, սուր ընդ մէջ եւ վահան ի ձեռին՝ ոչ միայն արանց քաջաց, այլ եւ կանանց առնականաց։

Իսկ գունդն Հայոց ամենայն աւգնականաւքն հան-դերձ եւ մոգացն բազմութեամբ յամսեանն չորրորդի եկին հասին յաշխարհին Հայոց, ի գիւղաքաղաք մի մեծ՝ որում ա-նուն էր Անգղ։ Բանակեցան, բոլորեցան, զետեղեցան, եւ յամենայն կողմանց անդր ժողովեցան, եւ էին անթիւ բազ-մութիւն։

Եւ եղեւ յետ աւուրց քսան եւ հնգից մոգպետն ինք-նին մոգաւքն հանդերձ հասանէր մեծաւ զաւրութեամբ՝ քակել զդրունս եկեղեցւոյն յաւուր միաշաբաթուն. զփորձ առնուլ կամէր զառաջարկութեան գործոյն։ Իսկ սուրբն Ղեւոնդ երէց միաբանութեամբ առաջին խորհրդակցաւքն եւ բազում ուխտիւ ի տեղւոջ անդ պատրաստական դի-պեցաւ։ Թէպէտ եւ ոչ էր տեղեկագոյն մտաց ամենեցուն նախարարացն, եւ ոչ զաւրութեան ուժոյ մոգպետին, ոչ ինչ եկաց մնաց ամենայն եպիսկոպոսացն, եւ ոչ առ սակաւ մի համբեր անաւրէն իշխանին թողացուցանել. այլ բազում ամբոխ աղաղակի զաւրացն եւ մոգացն հասուցանէր։ Քան-զի վիրգս ի ձեռն առեալ՝ զկառափունս մոգացն եւ մոգպե-տին ջարդեցին. փախստական յիւրաքանչիւր վանս արկա-նէին, եւ ինքեանք զպաշտաւնն բարձրացուցեալ յեկեղեց-ւոջն՝ զաւէրունական կանոնն կատարէին, մինչեւ ի նոյն միաշաբաթին անդադար լինելով։

Let wife fight against husband and servant turn against master. Divine law shall reign over all, and by the same law shall transgressors receive the punishment of condemnation."

When this was thus established, they appeared armed and helmeted, swords at waists and shields in hand—not only valiant men, but manly women also.

The army of the Armenians, with all its auxiliary troops and a crowd of magi, came to Armenia in the fourth month, to a large spot called Ang'gh, where they set up camp, settled and gathered from all sides to form a vast force.

And it happened after twenty-five days that the mogbed himself arrived with the magi and a great force to break open the doors of the church one Sunday, resolving to try the proposed deed. But the holy presbyter Ghevond, in brotherhood with his associates and many clergy, was present and ready. Although he was not informed about the intentions of all the nakharars, nor of the power of the mogbed's forces, he did not wait for all the bishops, nor did he suffer the impious ruler, but brought a huge uproar upon the troops and magi. For with staves in their hands they broke the skulls of the magi and mogbeds, causing everyone to flee their stations, and they resumed the Divine Liturgy at church for the rest of the Sunday.

CHAPTER III

Եւ յետ այսր տագնապի խռովութեան՝ յամենայն կողմանց յաշխարհէն Հայոց բազմութիւն արանց եւ կանանց ի տեղին հասանէին: Եւ անդ էր տեսանել զմեծ աղէտ տարակուսին. ոմանք զդեր արտաւսր արձակելով իբր յաղբերականց հոսէին յաչաց իւրեանց. այլքն բարձրաձիչ աղաղակաւ՝ իբր այն թէ զերկինս դողացուցանէին, իսկ կէսքն խիզախելով եւ ի զէնս ընթանալով՝ զմահ քան զկեանս ընտրէին: Իսկ ոմանք ի սուրբ ուխտէ եկեղեցւոյն՝ զաւետարանն ի ձեռն առեալ, աղաւթիւք առ Աստուած կարդային. եւ այլք ըղձանային զպատառումն երկրին, զի անձանց լիցի գերեզման: Եւ այսպէս շտապ տագնապի ի վերայ մոգպետին հասուցանէին: Բազում անգամ աղաչէր զաւգնականսն իւր, զի ի մահուանէ կարասցեն զնա ապրեցուցանել, եւ ողջանդամ անդէն յարքունիսհասուցանել:

Այլ վասն գործոյն յոր եկեալն էր՝ ստիպէր զնոսա եւ ասէր. «Թող գրեմ եւ ցուցանեմ մեծ թագաւորին, զի ի բաց թողցէ զայսպիսի իրաց առաջարկութիւն. զի եթէ եւ ինքեանք աստուածքն եկեսցեն մեզ յաւգնութիւն, չէ հնար աւրինացս մոգութեան ի Հայս առնուլ զհաստատութիւն. որպէս զփորձ առի զմիաբանութեան ուխտին եկեղեցւոյ: Զի թէ էին զաւրք աշխարհիս մոգք, ոչինչ խնայէին սոքա ի նոսա սատակմամբ՝ ոչ միայն զարտաքինսն, այլ եւ յեղբարս եւ յորդիս եւ յամենայն մերձաւորս իւրեանց, նաեւ ոչ յանձինս իւրեանց: Մարդք, որ ոչ ի կապանաց զանգիտեն, եւ ոչ ի տանջանաց երկնչին, եւ ոչ ի ստացուածոց պատկառին, եւ որ յետին չար է քան զամենայն չարիս՝ զմահ քան զկեանս ընտրեն, ո՞վ է, որ կարէ նոցա դիմակաց լինել:

After this tumultuous disorder, a multitude of men and women arrived at that place from Armenia. There was seen a great calamity of doubt; some burst into tears that flowed like fountains from their eyes, others cried loudly as though they would shake the heavens, and others braved, bearing arms, seeking death over life. Some among the holy faithful of the church took up the Gospel in their hands and prayed to God, while others wished that the earth would split open to become their grave. All this quickly brought torment upon the mogbed. Many times he begged his auxiliaries to rescue him from death and safely escort him back to the royal court.

But regarding the work for which he came, he pressed them and said: "Let me write and demonstrate to the great king that he should relinquish such an undertaking, for even if our gods themselves come to our assistance, there is no way for the customs of the magi to be established in Armenia, as I have tested the brotherhood of the faithful of the church. Even if the soldiers in the land were magians, [the Armenians] would not spare their destruction—not only foreigners, but also their brothers, sons and all their relatives, and even themselves. Who can oppose men who do not frighten of arrest, do not fear suffering, do not revere material gains, and eviler than all other evils, prefer death to life?

CHAPTER III

«Լուեալ իսկ էր իմ ի նախնեաց մերոց, եթէ յաւուրս Շապհոյ արքայից արքայի, իբրեւ սկսաւ ուսումն այդ աճել եւ բազմանալ եւ լնուլ զամենայն երկիրն Պարսից, եւ եւս անդր յարեւելս հասանել, իսկ որ վարդապետքն էին աւրինացն մերոց՝ յորդորեցին զթագաւորն, զի մի՛ բնաւ ամենեւին բարձցին աւրէնք մոգութեան յաշխարհէն, եւ հրաման սաստիկ, զի լռեալ դադարեսցէ քրիստոնէութիւն: Եւ որչափ նա կարճելով արգելուլ կամեցաւ, նոքա եւս քան զեւս աճեցին եւ բազմացան, եւ հասին մինչեւ յաշխարհն Քուշանաց, եւ անտի ի հարաւակողմն մինչեւ ի Հնդիկս տարածեցաւ:

Եւ այնպէս աներկիւղ եւ համարձակք էին յաշխարհին Պարսից, մինչեւ յամենայն քաղաքս աշխարհին եկեղեցիս շինեցին, որ զանցուցանէր պայծառութեամբ զթագաւորաբնակ արքունեաւքն: Շինէին եւ վկայարանս իմն անուանեալս, եւ զնոյն զարդ եկեղեցեաց զարդարէին, եւ յամենայն տեղիս անապատս միայնանոցս շինէին: Եւ իբրեւ ոչ ինչ երեւէր յայտնի աւգնութիւն ուստեք, աճելով աճէին եւ բազմանալով բազմանային, եւ մարմնաւոր մեծութեամբք մեծանային: Զպատճառս հարստութեանն մեք ինչ ոչ գիտէաք, բայց այսչափ ինչ ճշգրտիւ իմանայաք, զի տիեզերք ամենայն զկնի ուսմանց նոցա գնային:

"I had heard from our ancestors that, in the days of Shapur,[32] king of kings, when this doctrine began to spread and multiply throughout the whole land of the Persians, and also beyond to the East, the teachers of our doctrine provoked the king to issue a rigorous order lest the rites of Magianism be wholly extinguished from the land, and he gave a strong command that Christianity be silenced and abolished. Yet the more he resolved to forbid it, that much more did it spread and multiply, reaching into the land of the Kushans and to the south, and even to India.

[The Christians] in the land of the Persians were so fearless and bold that in all the cities of the land they built churches that surpassed the splendor of the royal palace. They built martyr shrines and adorned them in the same fashion as the churches, and in all secluded places they built hermitages. With no apparent help from anywhere, they increased and multiplied and prospered materially. The cause of this prosperity we know not; but this much we did know well: that the whole world was following their teaching.

32 Shapur II, 309-379.

«Թէպէտ եւ էարկ ի նոսա թագաւորն զձեռն իւր խստութեամբ, եւ զբազումս կալաւ եւ չարչարեաց ի նոցանէ, եւ զեւս բազումս մահուամբ սատակեաց, դառնացաւ եւ ձանձրացաւ յանձն իւր, եւ զնոսա ոչ կարաց նուազեցուցանել ի բազմութենէն: Դարձեալ թէպէտ փակեաց եւ կնքեաց զդրունս եկեղեցեացն ընդ ամենայն աշխարհն Պարսից, նոքա զամենայն տուն եկեղեցի արարին, եւ յամենայն տեղւոջ զիւրեանց աւրէնսն կատարէին, եւ զանձինս իւրաքանչիւր վկայարանս համարէին, եւ լաւագոյն զշինուածս մարդկեղէնս քան զհողեղէնսն հաշուէին: Սուրք սպանողացն բթեցան, եւ նոցա պարանոցքն ոչ ձանձրացան. աւարառուք ստացուածոց նոցա աշխատեցան, եւ աւարն աւր քան զաւր աճեցեալ բազմացաւ: Սրտմտեալ էր թագաւորն, եւ յոյժ դառնացեալ դահիճք բարկութեանն. իսկ նոքա արթունք եւ զուարթունք, եւ խնդալից ընդունէին զամենայն հարուածս տանջանացն, եւ սիրով տանէին զամենայն յափշտակութիւն ընչից իւրեանց:

«Իբրեւ ետես թագաւորն, եթէ գոռհ տուեալ դիմեցին ի մահ իբրեւ խաշինք սուրբք յաղն երկնաւոր, արգել եւ կարճեաց ի նոցանէ զհարուածս տանջանացն. եւ հրաման ետ մոգաց եւ մոգպետաց, զի մի՛ ամենեւին ոք խուեսցէ զնոսա, այլ հաստատեալ կայցեն աներկիւղութեամբ յիւրաքանչիւր ուսմունս, մոգն եւ զանդիկն եւ հրեայն եւ քրիստոնեայն, եւ որ այլ բազում կեշտք են ի կողմանս կողմանս աշխարհին Պարսից: Եւ ապա էառ երկիրն զխաղաղութիւն հաստատութեամբ, եւ լռեալ դադարեցին ամենայն խռովութիւնք յուզմանց: Քանզի ընդ մերոյ աշխարհին շարժման՝ եւ արեւմուտք եւս մեծապէս շարժեցան, եւ ամենայն Տաճկաստան ընդ նոսին խռովեցան:

"Although the king harshly extended his hand against them, seizing and torturing many of them, and exterminating many more, he became embittered and dejected, and could not diminish their growth. Although he closed and sealed the doors of the churches throughout all of Persia, they turned every house into a church and carried out their rites everywhere. Each person considered himself a martyr shrine and considered human buildings better than earthly ones. Their swords of their murders became blunted but their necks did not become weary; the plunderers toiled for their plunder but day by day the plunder multiplied. The king was furious and the executioners became much embittered with anger, but [the Christians] were watchful and sober, happily accepting all tortures, and gladly bearing all the plundering of their goods.

"When the king saw that the multitude approached death like a holy flock of the heavenly salt, he prohibited and cut short their tortures and commanded the magi and mogbeds to no longer mistreat them, but for each to firmly and fearlessly follow his own doctrine—magus and zandik [Manichean], Jew and Christian, and the many other sects all over the Persian empire. The land was established in peace and all disturbances and agitation ceased. For at the convulsion of our land, the land to the West was also greatly disturbed, and all of Assyria with it.

«Զայն ահա ի լսելոյ գիտեմք. բայց այս որ ես ինձէն աչաւք տեսի, թուի ինձ՝ թէ մեծագոյն եւս լինի քան զառաջինն: Արդ դու որ մարզպանդ ես աշխարհիս, պարտ է քեզ փոյթ յանձին ունել, գրել եւ ցուցանել յարքունիս զմիաբանութիւն բռնութեանս, ո՛րպէս աներկիւղութեամբ առ ոչինչ համարեցան զհրամանս արքունի: Եւ եթէ չէր մեր աճապարեալ եւ ի փախուստ դարձեալ, միում ի մէնջ ոչ տային ապրել: Եւ եթէ անզէն մարդիկ այդպէս բռնացան, եթէ յանկարծ զինուորս եւս ընդ ինքեանս միաբանեսցեն, ո՞ կարիցէ կալ առաջի դոցա յանդուգն յարձակմանդ:

«Ես ահա անտեղեակ էի անքակ ուխտի եկեղեցւոյդ ի միմեանց. զի ա՛յլ է՝ զոր լսէ մարդ, եւ այլ է՝ զոր տեսանէ հաստատուն իւրովք աչաւք: Դու որ ի մանկութենէ յայդմ ուրէնս սնեալ էիր, եւ ճշմարտեալ գիտէիր զպնդութիւն մարդկանդ, եթէ առանց բազում արիւն հեղլոյ դոքա մեզ ոչ տան ձեռն արկանել յեկեղեցիսդ, ընդէ՞ր զայդ ամենայն հաւաստեաւ յանդիման չասացեր ցթագաւորն: Քանզի ամենայն նախարարացն աւագ դու էիր, եւ զբոլոր աշխարհս քեզ յանձն արարեալ էր մարզպանութեամբ. ընդէ՞ր ոչ մեծապէս հոգ տարար յանձն քո: Զի յայլ ժամս իմաստուն էիր, եւ ես գիտէի. զայս գործ ոչ իմաստութեամբ գործեցեր: Ապա եթէ ոչ, յայտ է եթէ եւ դու ի նոցա բանի ես, եւ քոյով խորհրդով անցուցին զայս անցս ընդ իս եւ ընդ զաւրս:

"This we know from having heard it; but that which I have seen with my own eyes I reckon to be greater than hearsay. You [Vasak of Syunik], who are now the *marzban* of this land, are bound to write to the royal court regarding the strength of their brotherhood and how they fearlessly disregarded the royal command. Had we not hurried and fled, they would not have allowed any of us to survive, and if [these] unarmed people rose up like that, then who would be able to oppose their destructive assault if they suddenly were to unite with soldiers?

"I was ignorant of the indissoluble brotherhood of your church, for what a man hears is one thing, and what he sees with his own eyes is another. But you, who were nourished with these rites from childhood and truthfully knew the resolve of your people, that without much bloodshed they would not allow us to extend a hand upon their church, why have you not represented all this faithfully to the king? For you were senior among all the nakharars and the whole land had been given to you in your *marzbanate*—why didn't you take heed? At other times, you were wise, and I knew it, but in this, you acted without wisdom. If not, then it is clear that you are of their persuasion, and with your advice they brought these events to pass upon me and my soldiers.

«Արդ եթէ այդ այդպէս է, եւ քեզ կամք չէ ունել զմո-գութիւն, մի՛ ինչ պատկառեր դու երկիւղիւ յարքայէ. ես գրեմ եւ ցուցանեմ ի դուռն մովպետան մովպետի եւ դարանդար-ձապետի եւ մեծ հազարապետին, զի ածցեն զարքայ ի հա-ւանութիւն, որպէս զի ի բաց թողացուցէ ըստ առաջին հրամանին, եւ ի կամս մարդկան ապաստան արասցեն, զի առ սակաւ սակաւ ընդելցին ընդ աւրէնս մոգութեանս. զի որք կալցին՝ սիրով երեւեսցին կատարեալ զհրամանն ար-քունի: Քանզի մարզ է աշխարհս. գուցէ յորժամ վնաս ինչ առնիցեն, եւ ինքեանք ցրուեալ վատնեսցին յաւտարութիւն: Իսկ յորժամ աշխարհս թափուրլ ինիցի ի մարդկանէս, յայնժամ եւ քեզ գլխովին մեծապէս վիշտ հասանէ յարքու-նուստ»:

Ետ պատասխանի մարզպանն մոգպետին, եւ ասէ. «Ամենայն բանք խրատուդ զոր ասացեր՝ ճշմարիտ են. բայց զառաջինն զոր չիմացաք ՝ տեսեր, եւ մեծապէս զղջացաք այժմ: Բայց դու արդ զոր ասեմս արա, եւ բարիոք թուես-ցի քեզ. սակաւիկ մի երկայնամիտ լեր եւ զխորհուրդս քո արգել ի բազմաց. բայց արանց՝ որոց ես ասեմ՝ նոցա յայտնեա, մինչեւ ես ինձ ոյժ ժողովեցից՝ զաւր ի թիկունս ածելոյ, եւ զուխտ եկեղեցւոյդ թերեւս կարացից երկփեղ-կել: Եւ եթէ զայդ այդպէս արարից, գիտեմ ապա թէ եւ զհր-րամանն արքունի կարող եմ կատարել»:

"'Now if this be so, and if you do not resolve to hold to Magiansm, do not be ashamed of the king out of fear. I will write to the court, to the *Movpetan Movpet*, the *darandardzapet*, and to the great *hazarbed* [Mihr Narseh], to convince the king to free them from his former command and to let them act according to their will, so that they gradually make themselves acquainted with the Magian customs and so that those who come of their own accord will have fulfilled the royal command. For this land is a border province, and perhaps when they cause harm, they themselves will be scattered and lost to a foreign power. But if the country is deprived of its inhabitants, then great trouble will befall your head from the court."

The marzban answered the mogbed and said: "All the words of advice you spoke are true. You noticed that which we initially failed to perceive, and now we much regret it. But do as I say and it will seem good to you; have a little patience and keep your thoughts from the multitude, except for those to whom I tell you to reveal them, until I assemble a force for backup. Then perhaps I shall be able to break apart the faithful of the church. And if I can do that, I know that I can carry out the royal command."

CHAPTER III

Եւ անդէն հրոս հանեալ ի Սինեաց աշխարհէն, զիւր գունդն ստուարացոյց ի թիկունս ազնականութեան մոգաց եւ մոգպետին: Եւ ապա սկսաւ ասել. «Աղէ դու անգամ մի հրովարտակ ի դուռն տուր վասն այրուձիոյն՝ որ յԱղուանսն է տասն հազար, զի ի ձմերոց ի Հայս եկեսցեն. եւ յորժամ զնոսա ի ձեռին ունիցիմք, չիք ոք որ եղծանել կարէ զհրամանն արքունի»:

Պատասխանի ետ մոգպետն եւ ասէ ցմարզպանն. «Այդ խորհուրդ դարձեալ իմոց բանիցս ընդդէմ է. քանզի մեք յորժամ բռնութեամբ կռուեսցուք ընդ աշխարհիս, աշխարհս ի բաց քանդի, եւ մեք ի պատուհասէ չապրիմք. անձանց վնաս, եւ արքունի մեծապէս զեան»:

Եւ ոչ ինչ կամեցաւ ամենեւին ունկն դնել նմա մարզպանն, զի սրտիմտաւք կալեալ էր զպարսկական աւրէնսն: Սկսաւ այնուհետեւ պատրել զոմանս կարասեաւ եւ զոմանս ողոքական բանիւք. զռամիկն ամենայն՝ ահեղ բանիւք սպառնացեալ սրտաթափ առնէր: Հանապազորդ առատացոյց զռոճիկսն տաճարին, եւ յերկարէր զնուազսն ուրախութեան, մաշելով զերկայնութիւն գիշերացն յերգս արբեցութեան եւ ի կաքաւս լկտութեան, քաղցրացուցանէր ոմանց զկարգս երաժշտական եւ զերգս հեթանոսականս. մեծապէս գովութիւն մատուցանէր աւրինաց թագաւորին: Բերեալ էր եւ յարքունուստ բազմութիւն կարասւոյ, եւ միում միում կաշառ զաղտ խթէր ի պատճառս պարգեւի եւ պատուոյ. եւ բազում նենգութեամբ զանմեղ մարդիկ հրապուրէր եւ յինքն արկանէր:

Then taking troops from the province of Syunik, he increased the numbers of his own forces for the support of the magi and the mogbed, and he began to say: "Now send an order to the court that the horsemen in Aghuank, who number ten thousand, shall come to spend the winter in Armenia, and when we have them at hand, there shall be no one to fail the king's command."

The mogbed answered and said to the marzban: "This advice is contrary to my word, for by using force in this land we shall destroy it, nor shall we survive the calamity, which will result in harm to ourselves, and above all, detriment to the sovereign."

But the marzban would not hearken to all this, for he had heartily accepted Persian customs. He then began to deceive some with presents and others with flattering words, and he disheartened all the commoners by terrifying them with threats. He continually increased the budget of the temples, lengthened the songs of jubilation, extended the nights with drunken songs, licentious dances, music and heathen songs, and greatly praised the customs of the king. He had brought from the court much treasure, and one by one, he secretly bribed people on the pretext of bestowing gifts and honors. And with much cunning, he attracted innocent people to himself.

CHAPTER III

Իսկ զայս ամենայն իբրեւ տեսին սուրբ եպիսկոպոսունքն, եւս քաջ դրդեալ յորդորեցան ի նոյն միաբանութիւն. եւ հնարագէտ իմաստութեամբ ընդ երկուս բաժանեցին զբանակն: Մանաւանդ իբրեւ հաստատեալ գիտացին ի միտս իւրեանց, եթէ անաւրէն իշխանն Սիւնեաց զաւրհասական վէրսն ի յոգիսն ընկալեալ էր, խորշեցան մերժեցան եւ ի բաց փախեան ի նմանէ:

Խորհուրդ արարեալ ի գիշերի միում ամենայն ուխտին բազմութեամբ՝ կոչեցին եւ զսպարապետն զաւրուն ի խորհուրդն, հարցին եւ քննեցին եւ ի վերայ հասին մտացն անշարժութեան, որոյ ոչ եւ առ սակաւ մի թերացեալ էր ի սիրոյն Քրիստոսի: Եւ միաբան աղաւթս արարեալ ի վերայ նորա, վերստին ընկալան զնա յառաքինութիւն: Եւ նովաւ որսացան զբազումս ի նոյն միաբանութիւն, որք ոչ էին քակեալ յառաջին միաբանութենէն. եկին եւ ժողովեցան գունդ զաւրաց բազմաց: Եւ եւս առաւել հեռագոյն զատան ի մոգացն եւ ի մոգպետէն եւ յանաւրինէն Վասակայ:

Իսկ նա այնչափ յիմարեցոյց ափշեցոյց զմիտս մոգպետին, մինչեւ չետ նմա իմանալ զելս իրացն: Սկսաւ բաշխել մոգս ի տունս նախարարացն եւ մեծամեծ ռոճիկս կարգել, զոհել պատրուճակս, եւ բռնաբար կնքաւոր մարդկանն տալ ուտել միս յազածոյ, եւ երկիր պագանել արեգականն: Իբրեւ սկսաւ բազմանալ ընդ ամենայն աշխարհն այնպիսի պղծագործ խառնակութիւն, յանդգնեցան եւ եւս կանայք փշտիպանացն յաւուր կիւրակէի անցուցանել զճըրագունս եկեղեցւոյն եւ պատառել զհանդերձս հաւատաւոր կանանցն:

But when the holy bishops saw all this, they were all the more inspired and encouraged in their brotherhood, and wisely divided the army into two. Above all, when they figured out that the impious prince of Syunik had inflicted fatal wounds upon his own soul, they abhorrently turned away and fled from him.

Taking council one night all the clergy summoned the sparapet of the army [Vartan]. They questioned and examined him and learned of his firmness of mind, in which he had not in the slightest failed in his love of Christ. Having prayed for him together, again they received him in virtue, and through him attracted many into the same brotherhood, and those who had not forsaken the former union came and assembled, forming an army of many forces. Then they further distanced themselves from the magi, the mogbed and the impious Vasak.

But Vasak had so incited and stupefied the mogbed that he could not find a way to extricate himself. He began to distribute the magi among the nakharars' houses, to arrange great wages for them, to sacrifice animals, and to force those [who had been] baptized to eat sacrificial meat and to worship the sun. When such foul disturbances began to multiply throughout all the land, even the wives of the *pshtipans* dared to extinguish the church lights on Sunday and tear the clothes of the pious women.

CHAPTER III

Զայս գումկան աղմկի իբրեւ տեսին միաբան սուրբ եպիսկոպոսունքն, զաւետարանն ի ձեռն առեալ հասին եւ անկան առանց հարցանելոյ ի վանս սպարապետին ուր ժողովեալ էին զաւրքն Հայոց:

Համբարձին զձայնս իւրեանց եւ ասեն. «Աղաչեմք զձեզ զամենեսեան սուրբ աւետարանաւս. եթէ ձերով խորհրդիւ գործեն զայն անաւրէնութեան չարիս մարզպանն եւ մոգպետն, նախ զմեր պարանոցս հատէք, եւ ապա յեկեղեցին ձեռնարկեցէք: Ապա թէ առանց ձեր կամաց նոքա զայն չարիսն գործեն, այսաւր խնդրեսցի վրէժդ այդ ի նոցանէ»:

Իսկ որք էին ի ներքս ի վանս սպարապետին՝ յոտն կացին, միաբան համբարձին զձայնս իւրեանց առ Աստուած եւ ասեն. «Դու Տէր սրտագէտ ամենեցուն, ոչ ինչ պիտի քեզ վկայութիւն ի մարդկանէ. եթէ խոտորեալ իցեմք իքէն սրտի մտաւք, զայն դու ինքնին քաջ գիտես. այսաւր իսկ դատեա զմեզ ըստ մեղաց մերոց: Ապա եթէ հաստատուն կամք յուխտի սուրբ աւետարանիս, դո՛ւ Տէր, լեր մեր աւգնական այսաւր, եւ տուր զթշնամիսն ճշմարտութեան ի ձեռս մեր, զի արասցուք ընդ նոսա ըստ կամաց մերոց»:

Զայս իբրեւ ասացին, ամենեքեան զգլուխ զգետնի հարկանէին, եւ ողջունեցան յաւետարանէն եւ յեպիսկոպոսացն:

Իսկ մի ոմն ի նախարարացն որ անդր դիպեցաւ, էր ի նոցա խորհրդի, եւ ոչ միաբանեաց ընդ նոսա ի մեծ վկայութիւնն. եւ անդէն առ ժամայն ի նոցունց ի տեղւոջն քարկոծեցաւ, եւ ահ մեծ անկաւ ի վերայ ամենեցուն:

When the brotherhood of the holy bishops saw this deplorable outrage, they took the Gospel in their hands and went uninvited to the sparapet's base, where the army of the Armenians had assembled.

They raised their voices and said: "We all beg, by the Holy Gospel, that if by your counsel the marzban and mogbed have done this impious deed, you would first behead us and then undertake to destroy the church. But if they have wrought this evil without your will, then we ask you to call them to account today."

And those who were inside the sparapet's base stood up, concordantly raised their voices to God, and said: "O Lord, knower of all hearts! You require no testimony from men. If we stray from you in our hearts, you know it well. Judge us today according to our sins. But if we stand firm in the covenant of the Holy Gospel, O Lord, be our helper today, and deliver the enemy of truth into our hand, so that we may deal with them according to our will."

When they had said this, they put their heads down to the earth and were blessed with the Gospel by the bishops.

But one of the nakharars who was there in their council did not agree with their great oath and was stoned to death by them at that very place, alarming everyone.

CHAPTER III

Յայնժամ ամենեքեան ի նախանձ բարկութեան բրդեցան, մինչեւ ամենայն տեսողացն երիկամունքն դողային, որք առ ոչ ինչ համարեցանզպարգեւս արքունի, եւ առ ոտն հարին զհրամանս ահագինս: Ընթացան վաղվաղակի ի զէնս իւրեանց, վառեցան կազմեցան զգիշերն ամենայն, եւ ընդ ծագել արեգականն զգունդն յերիս մասունս բաժանեալ ի բանակն արկանէին: Գունդն առաջին յարեւելից կուսէ, եւ գունդն երկրորդ յարեւմտից կողմանէ, եւ գունդն երրորդ ի հիւսիսոյ կողմանէ, շուրջանակի ի մէջ առեալ փակեցին զբազմութիւն բանակին. եւ զբազումս կոտորեցին, եւ զեւս բազմագոյնս կապեցին զերեւելի մարդիկ, եւ արկին ի բերդս ամուրս ընդ իւրեանց իշխանութեամբ: Եւ զառ եւ զապուռ եւ զաւար բանակին ի մի վայր ժողովեալ պահէին իբր հրամանաւ արքունի:

Իսկ զմարզպանն ձերբակալ արարեալ, եւ միաբանէր ընդ նոսա երդմամբ՝ հաստատուն կալ յուխտին, զղջանայր զառաջին քակումն ի նոցանէ: Անկանէր ապաշխարութեամբ յոտս սուրբ եպիսկոպոսացն, եւ աղաչէր խաղապատելով՝ զի մի՛ մերժեալ ընկեսցի առ ի նոցանէ: Կրկնէր եւ երեքկնէր զանսուտ երդումն առաջի բազմութեանն ի սուրբ աւետարանն, գրէր եւ կնքէր զերդումն եւ կապէր զաւետարանէն. եւ աղաչէր՝ զի յԱստուծոյ խնդրեսցի վրէժխնդրութիւնն, եւ մի՛ նոքա մարդկաբար սատակեսցեն զնա:

Իսկ նոքա թէպէտ եւ հաստատեալ գիտէին զնենգաւոր կեղծաւորութիւն նորա, եթէ խաբէութեամբ դառնայ անդրէն ի հին մոլորութիւնն, ոչ ինչ փոյթ առնէին ձեռն արկանել ի նա վասն առաջին յանցանացն, այլ սուրբ աւետարանին թողին ի դատապարտութիւն:

At that point, everyone became inflamed with zeal and all the spectators' kidneys trembled. They considered the king's presents to be nothing and they stomped upon his frightful orders. They immediately ran to their weapons, organized themselves throughout the night, and at dawn they split their forces into three divisions and advanced upon the enemy's army: They surrounded and enclosed the multitude of the [king's] army, with the first division from the east, the second from the west, and the third from the north. They killed many, and seized most of the prominent men among them and imprisoned them in forts that were under their command. They gathered the plunder and booty of the army in one spot and guarded it as though by the king's command.

When they arrested the marzban, he agreed with their oath to remain firm in the covenant and repented for having previously separated from them. He fell at the feet of the holy bishops in repentance and pled and wept to not be cast aside from them. He repeated twice and three times an unbreakable oath upon the Holy Gospel before the multitude; he wrote and sealed the oath and tied it to the Gospel and begged that they ask God to take revenge, and not to kill him as a man.

And although they firmly knew of his cunning hypocrisy, and that he would deceitfully return to his former aberrance, they did not hurry to their hands on him on account of his former faults, and left his sentence to the Holy Gospel.

CHAPTER III

Իսկ որք եկեալ էին յաւարի առնուլ զսուրբ զանձս եկեղեցւոյն, ակամայ եդին զանձինս եւ զաւար իւրեանց առաջի սուրբ եպիսկոպոսացն եւ ամենայն զաւրացն. եւ եղծաւ ապականեցաւ հրաման թագաւորին: Եւ յաջողեալք զաւրութեամբն Աստուծոյ՝ աղաղակէին եւ ասէին գոհանալով արք եւ կանայք եւ ամենայն ռամիկ բազմութիւնն. «Պատրաստ եմք ի հալածանս եւ ի մահ եւ յամենայն նեղութիւնս եւ ի չարչարանս վասն սուրբ եկեղեցեաց, զոր աւանդեցին հարքն մեր առաջինք՝ զաւրութեամբ գալստեան Տեառն մերոյ Յիսուսի Քրիստոսի, որով վերստին ծնաք ի մի յոյս հաւատոցն մկրտութեամբ ի Քրիստոս Յիսուս. ըստ նմին նմանութեան կամիմք չարչարանաւք եւ արեամբ նորոգել զանձինս: Քանզի հայր մեր զսուրբ աւետարանն գիտեմք, եւ մայր՝ զառաքելական եկեղեցի կաթողիկէ. մի՛ ոք չար անջրպետ ի մէջ անկեալ՝ զմեզ քակեսցէ ի սմանէ»:

Ոչ երեւէր այնուհետեւ առաւել տէր քան զծառայ, եւ ոչ ազատ փափկացեալ քան զգեղջուկ վշտացեալ, եւ ոչ ոք քան զոք նուաղեալ ի յարութենէ: Մի սիրտ յաւժարութեան ամենեցուն արանց եւ կանանց, ծերոց եւ տղայոց եւ ամենայն միաբանելոց ի Քրիստոս: Քանզի առ հասարակ զմի զինուորութիւն զինուորեցան եւ զմի ագան զրահս հաւատոց պատուիրանին Քրիստոսի. միով գաւտեաւ ճշմարտութեան պնդեցին զմէջս արք եւ կանայք:

Ընկեցեալ կայր այնուհետեւ ոսկի, եւ ոչ ոք առնոյր իւր առանձինն արծաթ, եւ արհամարհեալ առանց ագահութեան, անարգեալ պատուական հանդերձք առ ի զարդս մեծարանաց: Նա՝ իւրաքանչիւր ստացուածք ոչ ինչ համարէին յաչս ստացողաց իւրեանց: Տեսանէին զանձինս իւրեանց իբրեւ զմեռեալ դիակունս, եւ զիւրաքանչիւր գերեզմանս ինքեանք փորէին, եւ կեանք իւրեանց ի մահ համարեալ էին, եւ մահք իւրեանց անշուշտ կեանք:

Those who had plundered the sacred treasures of the church were forced to surrender themselves and their spoils before the holy bishops and the whole army, and the royal order was nullified. Succeeding with the strength of God, the men, women, and the whole multitude of commoners cried out with gratitude and said: "We are ready for persecution and death and all troubles and torments for the holy churches, which were passed down to us from our forefathers by the power of the coming of our Lord Jesus Christ, through whom we were born again by the one hope of faith in the baptism of Christ Jesus. Likewise, we resolve to renew ourselves through torture and blood. For we acknowledge as our father the Holy Gospel, and as our mother the Apostolic Catholic Church. Let no evil separation come between us to detach us from her."

Thereafter, master seemed no greater than servant, nor softened noble greater than hardened peasant, nor was anyone weaker in courage than anyone else. One willing heart for all—men and women, old and young, and all those united in Christ. For they all become soldiers together and wore the same armor of faith in Christ's command, and with the same belt of truth, both men and women girded their waists.

Then gold was cast away and no one took up silver for himself, and without avarice they rejected precious clothing worn for fashion and honor because of their disdain for these things. Likewise, all possessions were considered as nothing in the eyes of their owners. They saw themselves as corpses, with each one digging his own grave; they considered that their lives were death, and that their deaths were assured life.

Բայց այս բարբառ ստէպ ստէպ ընթանայր. «Քաջութեամբ միայն մեռցուք, զանուն եւ զոգիս եւեթ ժառանգեսցուք, զի կենդանի իցէ ի մեզ Քրիստոս, որում դիւրին է միասանգամ նորոգել զմեզ ի հողոյ եւ զամենայն զյառաջագոյն զննջեցեալսն, եւ հատուցանել իւրաքանչիւր ըստ գործըս իւրեանց»:

Զայս եւ առաւել քան զոյնս խաւսելով, եւ մխիթարելով զանձինս եւ զմիմեանս, դարձեալ միասանգամ զինուորքըն պատրաստեցին զզէնս իւրեանց, եւ աղաւթականքն անդադար լինէին յաղաւթսն իւրեանց, եւ պահողքն ճգնէին ի պահս իւրեանց: Զայնք պաշտաւնէիցն ի տուէ եւ ի գիշերի անհատ էին ի սուրբ սաղմոսսն. ընթերցուածք աստուածային կտակարանացն ոչ երբէք առնուին դադարումն յամենայն ժամ. սոյնպէս եւ մեկնիչքն ի մխիթարութիւն երկնաւոր վարդապետութեանն:

Յայնմ ժամանակի դարձեալ յարձակեցան ի վերայ բերդիցն եւ աւանաց, զոր ունէին Պարսիկքն ի տեղիս տեղիս, յամրոցս աշխարհին. տապալէին քանդէին զբնակութիւն նոցա: Առաջին զմեծն Արտաշատհանդերձ աւանաւք իւրովք. եւ առնուին զանմատոյց ամուրսն՝ զԳառնի քաղաքն, զԱնին, զԱրտագերս եւ զաւանս իւրեանց. զԵրկայնորդսն եւ զԱրխնին եւ զաւանս իւրեանց. զԲարձրաբողն, զԽորանիստն, զԾախանիստն, զանկասկածելի Ողականն, եւ ընդ նոսա եւ զաւանս իւրեանց. զԱրփանեալն, զՎանն աւան, ընդ նմին եւ զաւանսն իւր. զԳռեալն եւ զԿապոյտն, զՈրոտն եւ զՎաշակաշատն:

But these words quickly proceeded: "Let us only die courageously, let us only inherit name and spirit, so that within us may live Christ, for whom it is easy to renew again out of dust, both ourselves and all those who expired before us, and to repay each according to his deeds."

Speaking of this, and more, and consoling themselves and each other, the soldiers once more prepared their arms, the prayerful prayed without ceasing, and the fasters devoted themselves to their fasts. The voices of the worshippers did not cease to sing the holy psalms day and night. Neither the readings of the divine testaments nor the interpreters of the consolation of the heavenly teaching ceased at any time.

Then again they attacked the forts and surrounding towns of the Persians in various secure places of the land and demolished and destroyed their dwellings. First, they took the great Artashat with its villages; then, they took the inaccessible fortress of the city of Garni, as well as Ani, Artakers and their villages; Yerkainort and Arkhni and their villages; Bardzrabogh, Khoranist, Tsakhanist, the indubitable Oghakan and their villages; Arpaneal, the town of Van and its [surrounding] villages; Kreal and Kapuyt, Orotn and Vashakashat.

CHAPTER III

Զամենեսին զայս իւրաքանչիւր գեղիք եւ ագարակաւք, զաւրաւք եւ զաւրագլխաւք ի նմին ամի առեալ տապալեցին, եւ ի գերութիւն վարեցին զարս եւ զկանայս ընչիւք եւ ստացուածովք, հանդերձ պատուական գանձիւք եւ նոցին սպասուք: Տապալէին քանդէին զշինուածս նոցա, եւ այրէին կիզուին զտունս պաշտաման կրակի: Սրբէին զպղծութիւն կռապաշտութեանցն, եւ առնուին զկահ եւ զկազմածս ատրուշանացն, բերէին եւ դնէին ի սուրբ եկեղեցւոջն, եւ ի ձեռն սուրբ քահանայիցն նուիրէին ի սպաս տէրունական սեղանոյն: Եւ փոխանակ սնոտի պաշտամանցն, զոր տապալեցին յամենայն տեղիս հեթանոսացն, զփրկական խաչն Քրիստոսի կանգնէին, զամենասուրբ սեղանն ուղղէին, եւ զկենդանարար խորհուրդն կատարէին սրբութեամբ. Պաշտաւնեայս եւ քահանայս ի տեղւոջն կացուցանէին: Յուսով հաստատեալ խնդայր ամենայն երկիրն առ հասարակ:

Եւ մինչդեռ յայսմ մեծի առաքինութեան կատարեալ գործէին զգործ նահատակութեանն, երեւէր իմն ի վերայ ամենեցուն աստուածային շնորհք. քանզի առանց հրամանի ի զաւրացն Հայոց, յարեւելից կողմանէ աշխարհին յարձակեցան ոմանք յԱտրպատական աշխարհն, եւ ի տեղիս տեղիս բազում վնաս արարին՝ առնլով եւ աւերելով եւ քանդելով զբազում ատրուշանս:

Իսկ որ ի մեծ ամուրսն անկանէին՝ խաչանշան արարեալ՝ ի վերայ զաւրուն յարձակէին. որ եւ երկու մեծամեծ բերդացն պարիսպքն առանց ուրուք մերձենալոյ անկեալ կործանեցան. մինչեւ ամենայն բնակչաց երկրին զահի հարեալ ի մեծ նշանէն, ինքեանք ինքեանց ձեռաւք զկրակատունսն այրէին. ուրանալով զաւրէնս մոգութեանն՝ խոստովանէին ի սուրբ աւետարանն:

All of these, including each one's villages and farms, troops and commanders, they took and destroyed in the same year, and took as captive men and women together with their riches and possessions, treasures and wares. They demolished and destroyed their buildings and burnt down their houses of fire-worship. They cleansed the impurity of idolatry and took the vessels and goods of the fire temples. They brought and placed them in the holy churches, and by the hands of the holy priests they consecrated them to the service of the Lord's altar. Instead of the vain offices of worship that they demolished in all places of the heathens, they raised the redeeming cross of Christ, prepared the most holy altar, performed the life-giving sacrament with holy reverence, and appointed deacons and priests. With firm hope, everyone in the land rejoiced together.

And while they carried out their work of nahatakutyun with great virtue, divine graces came upon them all—for without any command from the Armenian forces, some attacked the land of Atrpatakan from the east and inflicted much harm in diverse places, plundering, ruining and destroying the fire temples.

Those who fell upon the great strongholds made the sign of the cross and attacked the troops; the two ramparts of the great fortress fell and collapsed without so much as being approached. All the inhabitants of the land were so terrified by this great miracle that they destroyed the fire-temples with their own hands, denying the religion of Magiansm and confessing in the Holy Gospel.

CHAPTER III

Եւ այլ մեծամեծ աջողութիւնք կատարէին ի ձեռն զաւ-րականին. քանզի ուր ոչ էր ակնկալութիւն, եթէ զանուն Աստուծոյ ոք յիշեսցէ, արհաւիրք մեծ անկանէին ի վերայ նոցա, եւ ամենայն մարդ պատմէր ընկերի իւրում տեսիլս նորս եւ զարմանալիս: Սոյնպէս եւ աստեղք ի յերկինս երե-ւէին յոյժ լուսալիր պայծառացեալ, զոր ոչ ունէին յառաջին բնութեանն: Եւ ամենայն տղայք աշխարհին իբրեւ զարս պատերազմողս խիզախէին:

Եւ ահա յետ աւուրց բազմաց եկն եհաս հազարա-պետն Աղուանից սուրբ եպիսկոպոսաւ աշխարհին, մեծաւ տագնապաւ փութացուցանէր զզաւրսն ասելով. «Գունդն Պարսից, որ էր ի կողմանս աշխարհին Հոնաց, դարձաւ այսրէն, եկն եմուտ յաշխարհս մեր. եւ բազում եւս եւ այլ այրուձի որ ի դրանէ եկն: Եւ թող զայս ամենայն, այլ երեք հարեւր մոգ վարդապետ ածեալ ընդ իւրեանս, պառակ-տեցին զաշխարհն, եւ զոմանս ոմանս յինքեանս արկին, եւ կամէին յեկեղեցին ձեռն արկանել. եւ հրամանաւ թագա-ւորին ստիպէին զամենեսեան եւ ասէին. «Եթէ կամաւք յանձն առնուք զաւրէնսն, պարգեւս եւ պատիւս գտանէք ի նմանէ, եւ թողութիւն հարկացն յարքունուստ լիցի ձեզ, ապա թէ կամաւք զայդ չառնէք, հրաման ունիմք ի գեաւղս եւ ի քաղաքս շինել ատրուշանս, եւ զվռամական կրակն ի ներքս դնել, եւ կացուցանել մոգս եւ մոգպետս աւրէնսդիր ամենայն աշխարհիդ: Եւ եթէ ստամբակեալ ոք ընդդէմ դարձցի, ինքն մահու պատուհաս ընդունի, եւ կին եւ որդիք այնպիսւոյն անաշխարհիկ եղեալ՝ յարքունիս երթիցեն»:

Still more, great successes were accomplished by the army, for great fear befell the inhabitants in places where there had been no hope that anyone would recall the name of God, and everyone in these places related new visions and astonishments to his friends. Likewise, the stars in the heavens shone with greater brightness than formerly, and all the children in the land took courage like men of war.

After many days the hazarbed of the Aghuans came to the holy bishop of the land, and in great haste urged the army, saying: "The Persian army, which had been in the land of the Huns, has returned and entered our land with many additional troops and cavalry from the king. Besides this, they are accompanied by three hundred magian teachers and have divided the land, captured some people, and are determined to extend their hands upon the churches."

By the king's command the magi pressed everyone and said: "If you willingly receive the Magian religion, you shall find gifts and honors from the king and tax exemption from the court; but if you willfully do not receive our religion, we have an order to construct fire-temples in the villages and cities to light the fire of Vram[33] inside and to establish magi and mogbeds as legislators throughout your land. Should anyone resist, he shall be sentenced to death, and his wife and children will be exiled and sent to the royal estates inside, and magi and mogbeds shall be established as legislators throughout your land. Should anyone resist, he shall be sentenced to death, and his wife and children will be exiled and sent to the royal estates."

33 'Atash Behram' ("fire of victory"), the most sacred fire in the Zoroastrian religion.

CHAPTER III

Իսկ գունդն Հայոց իբրեւ լուաւ զայս գոյժ դառնութեան, ոչ ինչ թուլացեալ լքան ի քաջութենէն. այլ դարձեալ համագունդ ժողով լինէր ամենայն աշխարհին վասն գուժաբեր հրեշտակացն, որ հասին առ նոսա: Եւ միաբան քաջալերս տուեալ՝ արձակեցին զնոսա, զի առ ժամանակ մի զնոսա պատիր խաբէութեամբ կալցեն, զի խափանեսցին ի չար կամացն՝ չձեռնարկել ի սուրբ ուխտ եկեղեցւոյն իւրեանց. եւ ինքեանք զաւրութեամբն Աստուծոյ խորհուրդ ի մէջ առեալ՝ հնարիւք ելս իրացն խնդրէին:

Յայնմ ժամանակի զմի ոմն ի մեծ նախարարացն ի տոհմէն Գնունեաց՝ Ատոմ, ճեպով առաքեցին յերկիրն Արեւմտից, ցուցանել զայս ամենայն խորհուրդ զչարիմաց թագաւորին Արեւելից, միանգամայն եւ պատմել զիւրեանց քաջութիւն արութեանցն, զոր գործովք կատարեցին՝ առ ոտն հարկանելով զհրամանն ահեղ, եւ մեծապէս սաստակումն ի վերայ մոգացն հաստուցանել, խնդրել ի նմանէ աւգնականութիւն սատարութեան, եւ եթէ նա կամեսցի՝ նմա իսկ մտանել ի ծառայութիւն:

Եւ այս է պատճէն հրովարտակին, զոր գրեցին առ Թէոդոս կայսր.

When the Armenian army heard this bitter news, they did not weaken or give up courage; but everyone from the entire land assembled on account of the ill news of the messengers. And they all, being encouraged, saw the Persians off, so that for a time they might deal with them cunningly in order to hinder their evil intentions, lest they interfere with the brotherhood of the Church's faithful. In the power of God they took council to find means to overcome the problem.

At this time one of the distinguished nakharars from the house of Gnunik, Atom, was sent in haste to the West to indicate all the plans of the malevolent king of the East, and at the same time to make known their brave works—treading upon the [king's] dreadful command and bringing considerable destruction upon the magi—to request help and support from [Theodosius], and even to serve him, if he so wished.

This is a copy of the letter that they wrote to emperor Theodosius:

CHAPTER III

ՅՈՎՍԷՓ եպիսկոպոս բազում եպիսկոպոսակ-ցաւք իմովք եւ ամենայն զաւրաւք Հայոց, Վասակ մարզպան եւ Ներշապուհ Ռմբուեան հանդերձ սպարապետաաւ եւ ամենայն մեծամեծ նախա-րարաւքս առ մեծանուն Թէոդոս կայսր, բազ-մացի ողջոյն մեր առ քեզ եւ ամենայն զաւրաց քոց, որ խաղաղաւէր մարդասիրութեամբ ձերով տիրէք ծովու եւ ցամաքի, եւ չիք ոք յերկրաւորացս, որ ձերում անարգել տէ-րութեանդ ընդդէմ դառ-նայցէ:

Որպէս մեք իսկ ունիմք զանսուտ յիշատակա-րանսն զառաքինի նախնեացն ձերոց, ունելով զԵւրոպէ՝ անցին եւ տիրեցին եւ Ասիացւոց կողմանցն սահմանացն Սէիրայ մինչեւ ի կող-մանս Գադերովնի, եւ ոչ ոք գտաւ ստամբակ-եալ եւ ելանել ըստ ձեռն նոցա:

Եւ յայնչափ մեծ իշխանութեան՝ դաստակերտ մեծ եւ սիրելի զՀայոց աշխարհս անուանէին: Վասն որոյ եւ նախնին մեր Տրդատիոս յիշելով զառաջին սէրն ձեր, որ ի տղայութեան փախուց-եալ ի հայրասպան մարդախողխող հաւրեղբարցն իւրոց՝ ապրեալ սնաւ յերկրիդ Յունաց, եւ ի ձէնջ թագաւորեալ տիրէր հայրենի աշխարհիս, սոյն-պէս եւ զհաւատսն որ ի Քրիստոս՝ ընկալեալ ի սուրբ եպիսկոպոսապետէն Հռովմայ, լուսաւոր-եաց զխաւարային կողմանս հիւսիսոյ. զոր եւ այժմ կամին ի մէնջ կորզել հանել խաւա-րասէր որդիքն արեւելից:

Bishop Hovsep, together with many of my fellow bishops and the entire Armenian army, as well as Vasak the marzban and Nershapuh Rmbosian, together with the sparapets and all the distinguished nakharars, to the illustrious Theodosius caesar, many greetings from us to you and your whole army, who in peaceful benevolence rule the sea and land, and whose unimpeded dominion none on earth can oppose.

We have truthful records of your valiant predecessors who, having taken Europe, passed over and ruled parts of Asia, from the borders of Seir to Gaderown, and no one resisted or escaped their rule.

In such a great empire, they called Armenia a great and beloved territory. Thus, our ancestor, Trdatios,[34] *remembered your former affection, who as a child fled from his murderous uncles who had killed his father, survived, and was raised in the land of the Greeks. Having been made king by you he ruled over his ancestral land, and likewise receiving faith in Christ from the holy archbishop of Rome, he shed light on the darkness of the northern lands, which the darkness-loving sons of the East now resolve to take from us.*

34 Trdat the Great, 298-330.

Եւ մեք ի ձեր քաջութիւն արութեանդ խիզախեալ, էր ինչ, որ ընդդէմ դարձաք նոցա հրամանացն, եւ բազում այն է, որ արդ առաջի պատրաստեալ եմք: Ընտրեցաք զմահ աստուածպաշտութեամբ քան զկեանս ուրացութեամբ. եթէ դուք եւս ի ձեռն առջիք զմեզ, աՀա կրկին կենաց դիպեցաք եւ ոչ միանգամ մահու: Եւ եթէ սակաւիկ մի հեղգայք, գուցէ բազում եւ այլոց աշխարհաց հասանիցէ տապ բոցոյ սորա»:

Եւ իբրեւ յանդիման եղեն մեծի թագաւորին, եւ ընթերցան զգիր պաղատանաց Հայոց աշխարհին եւ զյիշատակարանս նախնեացն, բազում մատեանք ի մէջ եկեալ ընթերցան, որ զնոյն ուխտ հաստատութեան ի ներքս գտանէին:

Եւ մինչդեռ երանելին Թէոդոս հարցանէր զամենայն սինկղիտոսն, եւ հնարս իրացն կամէր գտանել խաղաղութեամբ, եւ հոգ տանէր մեծաւ յաւժարութեամբ, զի մի՛ եկեղեցիքն արեւելից յափշտակեսցին յանաւրէն հեթանոսացն, ի նմին ժամանակի անդէն վաղվաղակի հասանէր վախճան կատարած ի կենաց նորա, եւ կարի չար խափանումն լինէր գործոյն աւգնականութեան:

Եւ թագաւորէ փոխանակ նորա Մարկիանոս կայսր, եւ ի ձեռն վատթարարանց խրատտուաց իւրոց ծառայից, Անատոլեայ՝ որ սպարապետն էր, եւ Եղփարիոս ասորի,

Emboldened by your gallant bravery, we opposed their commands, and there are many more that we are ready to oppose. We have chosen death in godliness to a life in apostacy; should you extend a hand to us, we will have met life again and not at once death. Now if you tarry even a little, perhaps this blazing fire will reach many other lands.

When they came before the great king and read the pleading letter of the Armenian country and the records of their ancestors, many books were brought forth and read, in which they had found the same firm covenant.

Now while the blessed Theodosius was demanding the whole Senate to find peaceful means for this task, he took care with great inclination that the churches of the East not be seized by impious heathens, at which time the end of his life came suddenly,[35] and the work of [obtaining] assistance was cruelly hindered.

Then the emperor Marcian was enthroned in his place, and at the instigation of two wicked advisers among his servants—Anatolius, the general, and Eghparios, the Assyrian,

35 July 28th, 450.

երկոքեան անարգք եւ վատթար արանց, միանգամայն եւ անաստուածք, ի նոցա բանս ելեալ թագաւորն, ոչ կամէր անսալ միաբան ուխտին Հայոց, որ ամենայն ուժովն իւրեանց ընդդէմ կացեալ էին չարութեանն հեթանոսաց: Իսկ անարիս այս լաւ համարէր պահել զուխտն հեթանոսաց վասն մարմնական խաղաղութեանն՝ քան պատերազմակից լինել ուխտին քրիստոնէութեան: Վասն այսորիկ փութացաւ արձակեաց դեսպանս առ թագաւորն Պարսից զնոյն Եղփարիոսն, եւ եմուտ ընդ նմա յուխտ հաստատութեան՝ ձեռնթափ լինել ի զաւրացն Հայոց զաւրու եւ զինու եւ ամենայն աւգնականութեամբ:

Եւ իբրեւ այս այսպէս հաստատեցաւ, եւ հատաւ աւգնականութիւն յուսոյ նոցա ի մարդկանէ, դարձեալ սուրբ եպիսկոպոսքն քաջալերել սկսան զանձինս եւ զաւրսն Հայոց: Թէպէտ եւ հայէին յիւրեանց սակաւութիւնն եւ յերկոցունց թագաւորացն միաբանութիւն, ոչ ինչ վատասրտեալ դողային, այլ ըստ առաջին ուխտին խիզախէին եւ ասէին.

«Պատրաստ եմք ի սպանանել եւ ի մեռանել. դիւրին է Աստուծոյ սակաւուք զբազմաց գործ գործել, եւ անարգաւք զմեծամեծ իրս կատարել»:

Թէպէտ եւ ոչ ունէին թագաւոր առաջնորդ, եւ ոչ արտաքուստ աւգնական զաւրս յաւտարաց, սակայն անձանց առաքինութեամբ եւ սուրբ վարդապետացն մխիթարութեամբ՝ համագունդ ամենայն նախարարքն զաւրաւքն իւրեանց յիւրաքանչիւր տանէ ի մի վայր գային հասանէին վաղվաղակի. բազում եւ այլ այրուձի, որ յարքունի տանէ անտի էր:

both of whom were ignoble, evil and at once ungodly men—the emperor did not resolve to join in the covenant of the Armenians, who with all their power were opposing the malice of the heathens. But this weakling considered it better to keep his alliance with the heathens in the interest of physical peace than to fight in companionship with the Christian covenant. For that reason, he hurried and sent as ambassador to the Persian king the same Eghparios, with whom he entered into a firm alliance, surrendering personnel, arms, and all assistance against the Armenian army.

When this was done, and their hope of receiving human assistance was gone, the holy bishops again began to encourage themselves and the Armenian army. Although they beheld their meagerness and the union of the two kings, they were not at all disheartened or shaken, but took courage in their former covenant, and said: "We are ready to kill and be killed: it is easy for God to accomplish through few the work of many, and to accomplish great things through lowly men."

Although they did not have a king as leader, nor assistance from foreigners, yet by their own virtue and the consolation of the holy vardapets, all the forces of the nakharars from each house gathered together immediately, along with much cavalry from the royal house.

CHAPTER III

Եւ զամենայն զաւրսն յերիս գունդս բաժանէին:

Զգունդն առաջին տային ցՆերշապուհ Ռմբոսեան, եւ գումարէին զնա պահապան աշխարհին, մերձ ի սահմանս Ատրպատական աշխարհին:

Եւ զգունդն երկրորդ տային ի ձեռն Վարդանայ զաւրավարին Հայոց՝ անցանել ընդ սահմանս Վրաց ի վերայ մարզպանին Ճորայ, որ եկեալ էր աւերել զեկեղեցիսն Աղուանից:

Իսկ զգունդն երրորդ տային ի ձեռս Վասակայ իշխանին Սիւնեաց, որ ոչ ի բաց կացեալ էր յուխտէն հեթանոսաց ըստ ներքին խորհրդոցն իւրոց:

Ընտրեաց եւ էառ ընդ իւր՝ զորոց գիտէր զթուլութիւն հաւատոց նոցա.

Զիշխանն Բագրատունեաց զաւրաւքն իւրովք:
Զիշխանն Խորխոռունեաց զաւրաւքն իւրովք:
Զիշխանն Ապահունեաց զաւրաւքն իւրովք:
Զիշխանն Վահեւունեաց զաւրաւքն իւրովք:
Զիշխանն Պալունեաց զաւրաւքն իւրովք:
Զիշխանն Գաբեղենից զաւրաւքն իւրովք:
Զիշխանն Ուրծայ զաւրաւքն իւրովք:

Եւ զայլ բազում զաւրս յարքունի տանէն արկ յինքն, եւ զսեպուհս ոմանս յայլմէ տոհմէ: Եւ խորամանկ խաբէութեամբ դարանամուտ լինէր յամուրս իւրոյ աշխարհին, ի պատճառս կեղծաւորութեան՝ եթէ ընդ ճապուկ անդր անցանէ ի վերայ գնդին Պարսից՝ հալածականս առնել յաշխարհէն Աղուանից:

The entire army was divided into three regiments.

The first regiment was entrusted to Nershapuh Rmbosian, and assembled to guard the land along the border of Atrpatakan.

The second regiment was entrusted to Vartan, the general of the Armenians, to pass through the borders of Iberia and attack the marzban of Chor who had arrived to devastate the churches of Aghuank.

And the third regiment was given over to the hands of Vasak, the prince of Syunik, who had not disengaged himself from his alliance with the heathens in his inner thoughts, and selected as his soldiers those whom he knew to be of weak faith:

The prince of Bagratunik with his regiment.
The prince of Khorkhorunik with his regiment.
The prince of Apahunik with his regiment.
The prince of Vahevunik with his regiment.
The prince of Palunik with his regiment.
The prince of Gabeghiank with his regiment.
The prince of Urts with his regiment.

And he took many other troops from the royal house, and some junior nobles from other clans. Then with cunning deceit, he lay in wait in the fortresses of his land, under the pretext that from there he would flexibly fall upon the Persian army and drive them from the land of Aghuank.

CHAPTER III

Իսկ նա յամրածածուկ հաւալոցէն ճեպով դեսպանս արձակէր առ գունդն Պարսից.

> *Ահաւադիկ քակեցի զմիաբանութիւն ուխտին Հայոց, եւ ընդ երիս կողմանս զգունդն քակեալ բաժանեցի: Զգունդն առաջին հեռացուցի ի կողմանս Հերայ եւ Զարեւանդայ. եւ գունդս երկրորդ ընդ իմով ձեռամբ է, որոց ոչ ինչ տամ վնաս առնել զաւրաց արքունի: Եւ զայլ ամենայն, որ այր կռուոյ յաշխարհի աստ գտանէր, ցանեցի ցրուեցի ընդ ամենայն միջոցս աշխարհիս: Բայց զգունդն երրորդ արարի ընդ Վարդանայ յԱղուանս՝ սակաւաձեռն եւ ոչ բազմաթիւ: Ե՛լ համարձակ ընդ առաջ նորա, եւ մի՛ ինչ զանգիտեր ամենեւին տալ պատերազմ. գիտեմ՝ զի ի պարտութիւն մատնին առաջի քոյոյ մեծի զաւրութեանդ:*

Զայս գրեաց եւ եցոյց մարզպանին՝ որում անունն էր Սեբուխտ: Իսկ նա իբրեւ լուաւ զայս ամենայն զքաջալերս ի Վասակայ, եւ ստուգեալ հաստատեաց ի միտս իւր, եթէ սակաւաձեռն գնդաւ գայ սպարապետն Հայոց ի վերայ նորա, ոչ եկաց մնաց ի կողմանս Ճորայ, այլ կուտեաց զամենայն բազմութիւն զաւրու իւրոյ, եւ փութանակի անցանէր ընդ մեծ գետն Կուր անուն, եւ պատահէր նմա մերձ ի սահմանս Վրաց հանդէպ Խաղխաղ քաղաքի, որձմերոց էր թագաւորացն Աղուանից: Անցանէր բաւանդակէր ամենայն զաւրաւք իւրովք. ռազմ արարեալ զբոլոր մեծութիւն դաշտին ի ներքս փակէր. զինեալք եւ վառեալք ամենայն պատրաստութեամբ ի մարտ պատերազմի ընդդէմ գնդին Հայոց:

But from his secure hiding place, he quickly sent messengers to the Persian army:

> *Behold, I have dissolved the brotherhood of the Armenian faithful and divided their army into three parts. The first regiment I sent away to the region of Her and Zarevand; the second is in my hands, which I will not at all allow to harm the royal army. All the rest of the soldiery assigned here I scattered throughout the center of the land. But the third regiment I sent to Aghuank with Vartan, a poorly armed force, and not numerous. Go boldly before him, and do not hesitate to give them battle. I know that they will be worsted before your great force.*

This he wrote and showed to the marzban, whose name was Sebukht. When he heard these encouraging words from Vasak and verified and confirmed that the Armenian sparapet was marching upon him with a small contingent, he did not tarry in the region of Chor, but gathered his whole force, quickly crossed the great river named Kur, and happened upon [Vartan] at the border of Georgia, before the city of Khaghkhagh, which was the winter residence of the Aghuanian kings. Proceeding there with all his army, he manned the entire expanse of the field and blockaded the interior, being armed [and having taken] every preparation for battle against the Armenian army.

Իսկ քաջն Վարդան եւ ամենայն զաւրքն, որ ընդ նմա էին, իբրեւ տեսին զբազմութիւն պատրաստութեան գնդին հեթանոսաց, հայեցան եւ յիւրեանց սակաւութիւնն. թէպէտ եւ կարի յոյժ նուազունք էին քան զնոսա, ոչ ինչ զանգիտեցին առ ի յոյժ բազմութենէն, այլ առ հասարակ միաբան համբարձին յերկինս զձեռս իւրեանց, աղաղակէին եւ ասէին.

«Դատեա, Տէր, զայնոսիկ, ոյք դատին զմեզ. մարտիր ընդ այնոսիկ, որ մարտնչինս ընդ մեզ. Զին ու եւ ասպարաւ քով աւգնեա մեզ: Շարժեա եւ դողացո զգունդագունդ բազմութիւն անաւրինացս. ցրուեա եւ վատնեա զչար միաբանութիւն թշնամեաց քոց առաջի քոյոյ փրկական մեծի նշանիս, եւ տուր ի ձեռն սակաւուցս զքաջութիւն յաղթութեան ի վերայ անհնարին բազմութեանս: Ոչ ի պարծանս սնոտի փառասիրութեան անաւգուտ վաստակոց ինչ աղաչեմք, կամ յագահութիւն ընչասիրութեան զանցաւոր մեծութիւն կապտելոյ, այլ զի ծանիցեն եւ գիտասցեն ամենեքեան այնոքիկ, որ ոչն հնազանդին սուրբ աւետարանին քարոզութեան, եթէ դու ես Տէր կենաց եւ մահու, եւ ի ձեռն քո է յաղթութիւն եւ պարտութիւն: Եւ մեք պատրաստ եմք ի մեռանել վասն քո սիրոյդ. եւ եթէ սպանանել եւս հասանէ զնոսա, եղիցուք վրէժխնդիրք ճշմարտութեանն»:

Եւ զայս ասելով՝ խումբ արարեալ յարձակէին, եւ զաջ թեւն բեկեալ՝ զձախոյ կողմամբն արկեալ, սրոյ ճարակ զամենեսեան տային ընդ երեսս դաշտին, եւ փախստական առնէին մինչեւ յամուր տեղիս մայրեացն առ խորագոյն դարիւքն Լոփնաս գետոյ: Ուր ընդդէմ դարձեալ թագաւորազանց ոմանց Բաղասական արքայի, ընկեցին զոմն ի ձիոյ ի նախարարացն Հայոց, ի գնդէն Դիմաքսենից զՄուշ սպանին, եւ զԳազրիկ վիրաւորեցին:

When the brave Vartan and all his forces beheld the great multitude of the army of the heathens in array, they looked upon their own meagerness. Though they were much fewer than the Persians, they did not fear the great multitude at all, but all together they raised their hands to the heavens, cried out and said:

"Contend, O Lord, against those who contend with us; fight against those who fight against us! Rise for our help with your shield and buckler![36] Shake and tremble and defeat the great number of the unrighteous; scatter and waste the wicked union of your enemies before your great sign of redemption, and give into the hands of the few the power of victory over the huge multitude. Not for the boast of the fruitless rewards of vainglory do we pray, nor out of covetousness for seizing ephemeral greatness, but that those who do not obey the preaching of the Holy Gospel come to know this—that you are the Lord of life and death, and in your hands are victory and defeat. We are ready to die for your love; and should they be slaughtered, we shall become avengers of the truth."

Having said this, they split into groups attacked. Breaking the right flank, they set toward the left side, devoured by sword everyone over the open field, and drove them in flight to the strong part of the woods near the deep valleys of the Lopnas river. Here some of the royal troops of the king of Baghasakan returned and cast down an Armenian nakharar [who was] on horseback, killed Mush of the Dimaksian regiment and wounded Gazrik.

---

36 Psalm 35:1-2.

CHAPTER III

Յայնմ տեղւոջ դէտակն ի վեր ամբառնայր Արշաւիր Արշարունի, գոչէր առիւծաբար եւ յարձակէր վարազաբար, հարկանէր եւ սատակէր զՎուրկն քաջ զեղբայր թագուհին Լփնաց, եւ զբազում համհարզս նորին ընդ նմին սատակէր: Եւ այնպէս ամենեքեան առհասարակ այր զախոյեան իւր յերկիր կործանէր: Եւ առ յոյժ յանդուգն յարձակմանն յոլովագոյն այն էր զոր գետամոյնս առնէին քան զանկեալսն սրոյ ի ցամաքի: Եւ ի բազմութենէ դիականցն անկելոց՝ յստակ ջուրք գետոյն յարիւն դառնային, եւ ոչ գտանէր ոք ամենեւին ի նոցանէ ապրեալ եւ թագուցեալ յանտառախիտ մայրիս դաշտացն: Բայց մի ոմն ի զաւրականէ թշնամեացն՝ զինու համդերձ ելեալ ի նիւս երիվարին անցանէր ընդ մեծ գետն, մազապուր պրծեալ ի պատերազմէն՝ գոյժ տանէր ի մնացեալ բուն բանակն, որք փախըստական անկանէին ի մեծ շահաստանն:

Յայնմ ժամանակի զաւրքն Հայոց կատարելով զմեծ գործ պատերազմին՝ դիակապուտ դառնային, ժողովէին զբազում աւար բանակին, եւ կողոպտէին զանկեալ դիակունսն. եւ կուտէին բազում արծաթ եւ ոսկի, զզէնս եւ զզարդըս զարի արանց եւ զքաջ երիվարաց:

Դարձեալ յարձակէին ոչ սակաւ քաջութեամբ ի վերայ բերդիցն եւ քաղաքաց, զոր ունէին Պարսիկքն յաշխարհին Աղուանից, հզաւրապէս մարտնչելով այրէին զամուրս արգելանաց նոցա, եւ զերամս երամս մոգացն, զոր պատրաստական ածեալ էին աշխարհին գայթակղութիւն, ո՛ւր եւ գտանէին յամուրս ամուրս վայրացն, սրոյ ճարակ տուեալ՝ դնէին զէշ թռչնոց երկնից եւ գազանաց երկրի: Սրբէին զտեղիսն յամենայն պղծագործ զոհիցն, եւ փրկեալ ազատէին զեկեղեցիսն յանհնարին նեղութենէն:

There, Arshavir Arsharuni lifted his eyes, roared like a lion, attacked like a boar, and struck and killed Vurk, the valiant brother of the king of Lpink, and slaughtered many of his adjutants with him. Thus, everyone was felled to the ground by his foe and by the great boldness of the attack, many more drowned in the river than were cut down by the sword on land, and by the number of the fallen corpses, the clear water of the river turned bloody, and not a single one of them survived to hide in the dense forests of the plains. But one of the armed enemy soldiers got on horseback and crossed the great river, escaped the battle by a hair's breadth and delivered the sad news to those who remained from their camp, [many of] whom had fled to the great capital.

Then the Armenian army having completed this great battle, turned to despoiling the dead. They gathered much loot from the army, plundered the fallen corpses, and took much silver and gold, and the weapons and adornments of the brave men and their gallant horses.

Then, with no small valor, they attacked the forts and cities that the Persians held in the land of Aghuank, and fighting vigorously, set fire to their strongholds; and the flocks of magi who were prepared and dispatched to set snares in the land, wherever they were found in the strongholds, were devoured by the sword and fed to the birds of heaven and the brutes of the earth. They cleaned all those places from the impure offerings and redeemed and freed the churches from grievous trouble.

CHAPTER III

Եւ բազումք ի նախարարացն Աղուանից եւ յամենայն շինականացն, որք վասն անուանն Աստուծոյ ցրուեալ եւ վտանեալ էին յամուրս լերանց Կապկոհի, իբրեւ տեսին զաջողութիւն գործոյն, զոր կատարէր Աստուած ի ձեռն գնդին Հայոց, գային ժողովէին եւ նոքա, եւ խառնէին ի զաւրս նոցա, եւ միաբանք եւ հաւասարք կցորդք լինէին գործոյն նահատակութեան: Խաղային գնային այնուհետեւ ի վերայ պահակին Հոնաց, զոր ունէին բռնութեամբ Պարսիկքն. առնուին քանդէին զպահակն, եւ կոտորէին զզաւրսն, որ ի ներքս բնակեալ էին, եւ զդուռնն տային ի ձեռն Վահանայ, որ էր յազգէ թագաւորացն Աղուանից: Եւ յայսր ամենայն քաջութեան վերայ ոչ ոք անկեալ վիրաւորեցաւ ամենեւին ի նոցանէ, բայց ի միոյ երանելւոյ, որ կատարեցաւ նահատակութեամբ ի մեծ պատերազմին:

Եւ անդէն ի նմին տեղւոջ զայրն՝ որում զդուռնն յանձն արարին՝ զնոյն դեսպան արձակեցին յաշխարհն Հոնաց, եւ ի բազում յայլ ազգս բարբարոսաց, որ համագործք էին Հոնաց աշխարհին, բանս դնել ընդ նոսա եւ ուխտ հաստատել՝ անքակութեամբ ունել զմիաբանութիւնն: Իսկ նոքա իբրեւ զայն ամենայն լուան, փութապէս վաղվաղակի հասանէին ի տեղին, եւ ականատեսք լինէին գործոյն յաղթութեան: Եւ ոչ ինչ յապաղեցին երդմամբ յուխտ մտանել ըստ կարգի իւրեանց աւրինաց, յանձն առին եւ զերդումն քրիստոնէից՝ պահել ընդ նոսա հաստատութեամբ զմիաբանութիւն:

When many of the Aghuanian nakharars and all the peasants—who for the sake of God's name had scattered and dispersed to the strongholds of the mountains of Kapkoh—saw the success that God had accomplished through the hands of the Armenian army, they assembled and mingled with the troops, and in union and as equals partnered with them in the work of nahatakutyun. Thereafter, they went to the Gate of the Huns, which the Persians held by force. They destroyed the fortress, killed the troops within, and gave over the fortress into the hands of Vahan, who was [descended] from the royal line of Aghuank. None of them were wounded throughout all these brave exploits, except for one blessed man who was martyred in the great battle.

From there they sent the man to whom they gave the fortress as ambassador to the land of the Huns, and many other barbarous nations who were in alliance with the Huns, to agree to establish a pact to enter an indissoluble union. And when they [the Huns] heard about all that had happened, they hastened to the spot and beheld the victorious deed with their own eyes. They did not delay at all in pronouncing an oath according to their customs, and took the oath of the Christians to remain firm in their brotherhood.

Իսկ իբրեւ զայս կատարեցին եւ արարին իւրեանց մեծապէս հաստատութիւն, եւ դեռ անդէն ի տեղւոջն զե-տեղեալ էին խաղաղութեամբ, գուժկան հասանէր յաշխար-հէն Հայոց, զճակատ հարեալ եւ զաւձիս պատառեալ վասն ապստամբին Վասակայ. «Յետս կացեալ յուխտէն քրիստո-նէութեան եւ աւերեալ զբազում տեղիս Հայոց աշխարհին, մանաւանդ զձմերոցս արքունի, որ կայանք զաւրացն էին, զԳառնին եւ զԵրամաւնս եւ զԴրասխանակերտն՝ զմեծ դաս-տակերտն, զՎարդանաշատն եւ զամուրն Աւշական, զՓա-ռախուտն, զՍարդեանսն, զՁողակերտն աւան եւ զբերդն Արմաւրի, զԿուաշն աւան, զԱրուճն, զԱշնակն եւ զամե-նայն ոտն Արագածու, եւ զնահանգն Արտաշատու եւ զԱրտաշատն ինքնին գլխովին, եւ զամենայն գեւղս եւ զա-ւանս, որ շուրջ զնովաւ էին, առեալ աւերեալ եւ հրձիգ արարեալ, եւ զամենեցուն ձեր զընտանիս փախուցեալ մերժեալ յիւրաքանչիւր բնակութենէ: Ձեռն արկեալ եւ ի սուրբ եկեղեցիսն, տարեալ եւ զսուրբ սպաս եկեղեցւոյն սեղանոյ. գերի վարեալ զընտանիս քահանայից, եւ զնո-սին կապեալ եւ եդեալ ի բանդի. եւ ինքն սփռեալ տարած-եալ ասպատակաւ աւերէ զերկիրն ամենայն: Եւ գունդն, որ էր ի կողմանս Ատրպատականի, ոչ ժամանեաց ձեռն տալ ի միջոց աշխարհին: Եւ զաւրքն, որ անդ մնացեալ էին, խոյս տուեալ յանաւրինէն մերժեցան յեզր աշխարհին, եւ դեռ պահեն ընդ ձեզ զուխտ միաբանութեան սիրոյն Քրիստոսի: Բայց այն որ ընդ նմայն էին՝ են ոմանք, որ փախեան յիւրաքանչիւր տեղիս, եւ բազումք այն են, որ զհետ մոլորեցան նորա ամբարշտութեանն»:

When they concluded and confirmed this, and while they were at that spot in peace, messengers arrived in a hurry from the land of the Armenians with sad news regarding the apostate Vasak: "He has turned back from the Christian covenant and laid waste many places in the land of the Armenians, particularly the royal winter residences, which were stations for the soldiers, and Garni, Yeramon, the great estate of Draskhanakert, Vartanashat and the fortress of Oshakan, Parakhot, Sartean, the village of Tsokhakert and the fortress of Armavir, the village of Kuash, Aruch, Ashnak and all the foothills of Mount Aragats, the province of Artashat, Artashat itself, and all the villages and districts surrounding them he plundered and burned, and everyone in your families were forced to flee from their houses. He extended his hands upon the holy churches and took the holy altar vessels. He carried off the families of captive priests, and bound and imprisoned them. He spread corruption and ruin throughout the entire land. The army that was in the region of Atrpatakan was unable to assist in the interior of the country on time, and the soldiers who had remained there withdrew from the ungoldy [Vasak] to the borders of the land, where they still kept their covenant with you in unity with the love of Christ But those who were with [Vasak] included some who fled to their own places, but many more were led astray due to his impiety."

CHAPTER III

Զու արարեալ ի տեղւոջէ անտի՝ դառնալ անդրէն յաշխարհին Հայոց մեծաւ ստիպով եւ բազում աւարաւ եւ անչափ մեծութեամբ, եւ անտրտում ուրախութեամբ երգս ի բերան առեալ եւ աւէին ձայնիւ. Խոստովան եղերուք Տեառն, զի բարի է, զի յաւիտեան է ողորմութիւն նորա. ո՛ եհար զազգս մեծամեծս եւ սպան զիշխանս հզաւրս, զի բարի է, զի յաւիտեան է ողորմութիւն նորա: Եւ զայս սաղմոս երգելով մինչեւ ի վախճան կատարեալ աղաւթիւք փառատրութիւն սուրբ Երրորդութեանն մատուցանէին: Անդ յանձանձէր ածէր զաւրավարն զկաց եւ զմնաց զաւրականին առաջապահաւք եւ վերջապահաւք, կողմապահաւք ողջ եւ առողջ հասուցեալ յաւուրս երեսուն մերձ ի սահմանս հայրենի աշխարհին:

Ազդ եղեւ ուրացեալն Վասակայ եւ իշխանացն որ ընդ նմա էին՝ քաջութիւն նահատակութեան գնդին Վարդանայ յաշխարհին Աղուանից, եւ միաբանութիւնն եւս Հոնաց: Մինչեւ յանդիման եղեալ էին միմեանց, զգիշեր մի ազնական գտեալ նորա՝ փախստեայ անկանէր յամուրս իւրոյ աշխարհին. եւ այնպէս տագնապաւ մերժեցաւ, զգերի եւ զաւարն զոր առեալ էր յԱյրարատ գաւառէ, ակամայ զիւրն եւս ի վերայ եթող եւ փախեաւ:

Եւ քանզի ժամանակ ձմերայնւոյ հասեալ էր, եւ զոռճիկս՝ թշնամեաց գնդին հարեալ էր, ոչ կարէր զմիով տեղեաւ համագունդ զաւրսն դարմանել. այլ սփռէր տարածանէր ընդ գաւառս գաւառս աշխարհին առ ի հանգիստ ձմերոցին: Պատուէր հրամանի տայր պատրաստական լինել կազմութեամբ առժամանակ գարնայնոյն: Եւ զսակաւ ի գնդէն յաւագ նախարարացն գործակից իւր թողեալ, բնանայր ի վերայ՝ ունելով զթագաւորանիստ տեղիսն:

[The Armenian army] departed from there and returned to Armenia in great haste and with much loot and immeasurable riches, and with unmitigated joy they sang: 'Praise the Lord for He is good, for His mercy endures forever; He struck down many nations and killed mighty rulers, for He is good, for His mercy endures forever.'[37] And singing this Psalm to its end, they prayed in exaltation to the Holy Trinity. The general gathered together the soldiers that followed and posting watchmen in the front, rear and flanks of the army, they arrived in good health after thirty days near the borders of their native land.

News of the valiant nahatakutyun of Vartan's regiment in Aghuank and of their union with the Huns reached the apostate, Vasak, and the princes who were with him. Before they were to encounter each other, he took advantage of nightfall and fled to the strongholds of his land [Syunik]; leaving in haste, he even unwillingly left behind the captives and loot that he had taken from the district of Ayrarat.

Now because winter had arrived, and the enemy troops had taken the rations, he [Vartan] could not support his whole army in one place; rather, he spread them across the several provinces of the land for their winter quarters, and commanded all things to be prepared for the spring. Taking a few from among the legion of the senior nakharars as his associates, he strengthened himself by capturing and holding the royal districts.

37 Psalm 117:1; Psalm 117:10.

CHAPTER III

Եւ գունդս գունդս արձակէր յաշխարհն Սիւնեաց, առնոյր եւ աւերէր զբազում գաւառս. եւ այնպէս ի նեղ արկանէր զնա եւ զամենայն զաւրսն որ ընդ նմա էին, զի զէշս եւ զձիս մեռեալոտիս առ սովոյն վտանգի անխտիր ուտէին: Եւ բազում հարուածս հասուցանէր ի վերայ ուրացելոյն. մինչեւ ժողով սուրբ եպիսկոպոսացն եւ ամենայն ուխտ քահանայութեանն դառնապէս արտասուս իջուցանէին ի վերայ չարաչար վշտացելոցն, որ բոկ եւ հետի վարէին զարս եւ զկանայս փափկասունս, եւ բազում տղայք զքարի հարեալ ընկեցան յանցս ճանապարհաց:

Իբրեւ այս ամենայն աջողութիւն լինէր երկիւղածացն Աստուծոյ, ամենայն եպիսկոպոսունք եւ երիցունք պատուէր հրամանի տուեալ աշխարհին, զողջոյն ամիսն Քաղոց պահաւք եւ աղաւթիւք առնել խնդրուածս առ Աստուած, եւ զտաւն պատերազմացն յաղթութեան խառնել ի սուրբ տաւն յայտնութեանն Քրիստոսի, զի անխափան կացցէ մեծ յիշատակարանս այս ընդ աստուածային անանց տաւնին:

Եւ զսոյն զայս ամենայն այցելութիւնս Աստուծոյ, որ ի վերայ աշխարհին Հայոց մեծապէս երեւեցաւ, գրեցին սուրբ եպիսկոպոսունքն եւ ետուն տանել յաշխարհն Յունաց ի մեծ քաղաքն առ սուրբ ուխտ եկեղեցւոյն. զի եւ նոքա աղաւթս առնելով խնդրեսցեն յԱստուծոյ, որպէս սկսաք ի նմին եւ կատարեսցուք:

Vartan sent legion after legion to Syunik. He captured and laid waste to many provinces, and thus troubled Vasak and all the forces who were with him so much that they started eating the flesh of dead donkeys and horses from the danger of famine. Vartan dealt many blows to the apostate, to the point that the assembly of holy bishops and all the clergy shed bitter tears upon their grievous sufferings, which caused men and delicate women to go barefoot and many children to be dashed in pieces along the way.

When all these successes occurred for those who feared God, all the bishops and priests issued an order in the land to pass the whole month of Kaghots[38] in petitioning God with fasting and prayer, and to celebrate the victory of the war on the holiday of the Epiphany of Christ, so that this great memorial would be unimpeded by this divine and eternal festival.

All these visitations of God that appeared greatly in the land of the Armenians were recorded by the holy bishops and sent to the land of the Greeks to the holy clergy at the great city,[39] so that by praying they might entreat God to help us accomplish the work as we had begun it.

38 *Kaghots:* December.

39 Constantinople.

CHAPTER III

Եւ զոմն յառաջին կապելոցն Պարսկաց լուծեալ եւ ածեալ զառաջեաւ նախարարացն, խաւսէին ընդ նմա եւ ցուցանէին զամենայն վնասն որ եղեւ, կամ աշխարհացն աւերել, կամ զաւրացն արքունի հարկանել, եւ կամ որ այլ իրք առաջոյ լինելոց էին: Եւ իբրեւ զայս ամենայն բովանդակ ցուցին նմա, միաբան լինէր ամբաստանութիւն երկոցունց կողմանցն՝ զառաքինեացն եւ զյետս կացելոցն. ո՞րպէս զուր եւ տարապարտուց նեղեաց զնոսա ի հայրենի աւրինացն յետս կալ, եւ զխաբէութիւն ապստամբին Վասակայ, որպէս Հայոց բանիւ խաբեաց զթագաւորն, յանձն առնուլ զմոգութիւն. իբրեւ չէր ուրուք ընդ նմա բանս եղեալ, նա յանձնէ սուտակասպաս լինէր:

Իբրեւ լիով զայս ամենայն իմացուցին, արձակեցին զնա հրեշտակութեամբ յաղերս ապաքանութեան եւ ի հնարըս հայթայթանաց, թերեւս կարասցեն զեղբարս իւրեանց ի նեղութենէն գողանալ:

Այլ առ նա՝ անաւրէնն Վասակայ գուժկանքն յառաջագոյն հասեալ էին, պատմել զաղէտս տարակուսանացն, զոր անցուցեալ էր ընդ զաւրսն արքունի. Եւ ամենայն ամբաստանութիւնն ի սուրբ ուխտ եկեղեցւոյն կրթեալ էր: Քանզի այն իսկ կամք էին անաւրինին, եթէ զմիաբանութիւն եպիսկոպոսացն քակտեսցէ ի նախարարացն. եւ զայս ոչ էր տեղեկացեալ տակաւին, եթէ հոգի եւ մարմին բաժանիցին առ ժամանակ մի՝ զոյ տեսանել ի բնութեանս, այլ որ սիրովն Աստուծոյ յուխտ մտեալ է՝ այսմ անհնար է լինել:

Having released one of the foremost Persian prisoners and bringing him before the nakharars, they spoke with him and indicated all the harms that had occurred: the destruction of their lands, the defeat of the royal army, and all that was yet to ensue. When they demonstrated all this to him, he minded the accusations of both sides, the virtuous ones and those who stayed back; how vain and groundless was the endeavor to deprive them of their ancestral customs, and the deceit of the rebel Vasak, speaking [on behalf] of the Armenians and duping the [Persian] king that they would accept Magiansm. For while no one had agreed with him, he had become a sycophant of his own accord.

When they made all this abundantly clear, they sent him as a messenger [to the king] to make a plea and to try to find a means by which to deliver their brothers from straits.

But the messengers of the lawless Vasak had already reached [the Persian king] with the sad news of the catastrophe [Vartan] had brought upon the royal army, and laid all the blame upon the holy covenant of the church. For it was the will of the lawless [Vasak] to dissolve the brotherhood of the bishops and the nakharars. But he was not yet aware that the soul and body can separate temporarily, as can be seen in nature, but for those who join the community of the faithful out of their love for God, this is impossible.

CHAPTER III

Արդ երթեալ այրն ի տեղի ձմերոցին, պատմեաց զայս ամենայն յականջս թագաւորին, շարժեալ դողացոյց, որ եւ յամենայն զաւրութենէն պակասեալ գտաւ. մանաւանդ զի յարեւելից պատերազմէն կորակոր եւ ոչ բարձրագլուխ էր դարձեալ: Իբրեւ ստուգեալ հաստատեաց ի վերջին հրեշտակէն, որ եհաս առնա, զամենայն վնասս զիւր գործոցն զխորհրդակցաւքն արկանէր: Եւ անդէն շիջանէր ի բազմաբոց բորբոքմանէն. քանզի խցաւ բերան չար խրատտուացըն, որ անդադար յորդորէին զնա ի գործ դառնութեան: Խոնարհեցաւ ի բարձր հպարտութենէն, եւ զվայրենացեալ սիրտն դարձոյց ի մարդկային բնութիւն. հայեցաւ եւ ետես զինքն լի տկարութեամբ. գիտաց եթէ զամենայն զոր կամի առնել՝ ոչ կարէ կատարել. վասն այնորիկ եւ դադարեաց յանդուգն յարձակմանէն, եւ լռեցոյց զմոլեգնոտաբար գոչումնն:

Եւ որ մեծաձայն բարբառով որոտայր, եւ եւս ահագին հրամանաւքն զհեռաւորս եւ զմերձաւորս դողացուցանէր, սկսաւ քաղցր եւ աղերս բանիւք խաւսել ընդ ամենեսեան եւ ասել:

«Զի՞նչ ինչ վնաս գործեալ է իմ, եւ զո՞ր յանցս յանցուցեալ կամ առ ազգս կամ առ լեզուս կամ առ անձն իւրաքանչիւր: Ո՞չ ահա բազում ուսմունք են յաշխարհիս Արեւաց, եւ իւրաքանչիւր պաշտամունք յայտնի են. ո՞ երբէք նեղեաց պնդեաց դարձուցանել ի մի աւրէնս մոգութեան. մանաւանդ վասն աւրինաց քրիստոնէութեանն, որպէս հաստատուն եւ ճշմարիտ կացեալ են յիւրեանց դենին, նոյնպէս եւ առ մեզ լաւագոյն քան զամենայն կեշտսն նոքա երեւեալ են: Եւ բիծ իսկ ոչ կարէ ոք դնել ընտրեալ աւրինաց նոցա. այլ զոյգ եւ հաւասար համարիմ դենին մազդեզանց, որպէս եւ յարգեալ իսկ էին նոքա առ նախնեաւքն մերովք, զոր ես ինձէն իսկ յիշեմ առ հարբն իմով, որ նստէր ի մեծ գահոյս յայսմ:»

So that man [the messenger] went to the king's winter quarters and explained all this in his ear, which made him shake and tremble and made all his strength diminish, especially because he had returned from the war in the East ashamed and humiliated. When the king confirmed the news from this last messenger who had come to him, he blamed his advisors for all the harms [that had resulted] from his undertakings. Then he extinguished his ardent rage, for the mouths of his evil advisers, who had unceasingly provoked his bitter works, had been stopped. His haughtiness was humbled, and his brutish heart returned to its human nature; he looked and saw himself as full of weakness; he realized that he could not accomplish all that he had wished. Thus, he discontinued his headstrong attack and subsided and silenced his furious roars.

And he who had thundered with his loud voice and shaken those far and near with his more formidable commands began to address everyone with sweet and pleading words:

"What harm have I done? What transgressions have I committed against any nation, or people, or any person? Are there not numerous doctrines in the empire of the Aryans, and their services observed openly? Who has forced or pressed them to convert to the one religion of Magianism? Especially the Christian religion—as firmly and truthfully as they have stood by their creed, likewise have they have appeared to us as better than all other sects. No one can put a blemish on their religion; rather, I hold it to be equal with the religion of Mazdaism, as respected even by our ancestors, which I myself remember from my own father[40] who sat on this great throne.

40 Bahram V (420-438).

«Յորժամ սկսաւ անդաճել եւ քննել զամենայն ուսմունս եւ հաստատութեամբ ի վերայ եհաս, առաւել վեհ գտանէր զաւրէնս քրիստոնէից քան զամենեցուն. վասն այսորիկ մեծարեալք շրջէին ի Դրան արքունի, եւ առատաձեռն պարգեւաւք երահիկք լինէին ի նմանէ, եւ համարձակութեամբ շրջէին ընդ ամենայն երկիր: Նա եւ որ գլխաւորքըն էին քրիստոնէից, զոր եւ եպիսկոպոս անուանեն, ընծայից եւ պատարագաց արժանիս առնէր զնոսա: Եւ իբրեւ հաւատարիմ ոստիկանս յանձն առնէր նոցա զհեռաւոր մարզսն, եւ ոչ երբէք սխալ լինէր ի մեծամեծ իրացն արքունի:

«Եւ դուք զմի զայն երբէք ոչ յիշեցէք, այլ հանապազաւր ձանձրացուցէք զլսելիս իմ, խաւսելով զնոցանէ զամենայն չարութիւն: Տեսէք՝ զի ետուք գործել ինձ զոր ինչ ոչ կամէի, եւ եղեն վնասք մեծամեծք ի սահմանսն ի մէջ երկուց անհաշտ թշնամեաց: Եւ մեք դեռ ի հեռաւոր ճանապարհի, եւ ոչ մի ինչ գործ պատերազմիս ի գլուխ երթեալ, եւ դուք աստէն յիմում տանս յարուցէք ի վերայ իմ պատերազմ, որոյ չարագոյն եւս լինելոց է կատարածն իւր քան զարտաքին թշնամեացն»:

Զայս ամենայն եւ առաւել քան զսոյն խաւսէր ընդ ամենայն աւագանին, եւ զվնասս յանցանացն արկանէր զմոգպետաւն եւ զմոգաւքն: Եւ ամենայն վզուրկքն եւ պատուական նախարարքն, որ նստէին յատենին եւ ունկն դնէին յեղյեղուկ լեզուի նորա, ամաչեցեալ կորանային եւ ընդ երկիր պշնուին, եւ զգլուխի վեր ոչ կարէին համբառնալ:

"When he began to examine all doctrines and was firmly apprised, he found the Christian religion to be pre-eminent. Therefore, they were honored at the royal court, and were exalted by [the king] with lavish gifts, and fearlessly went about all the land. The leaders among the Christians, whom they called bishops, were dignified with offerings and gifts. And as his faithful officers he gave them possession of his distant border provinces, and never was there a fault in [their management of] the great affairs of the empire.

"You never recalled even one of these facts, but have incessantly wearied my ears by speaking of all their evils. Now see that you have made me do what I desired not to do, and there occurred great harm at the borders between two irreconcilable enemies, and while we were on a journey and could not carry out a war, you raised war upon me here in my house, which will end worse than the wars with our foreign enemies."

This and more he said to all the grandees and laid the fault upon the mogbeds and magi. And all the great and honorable nobles who were sitting in the council and heeding his deceitful words were brought to shame; they cast their gaze to the ground and could not lift up their heads.

CHAPTER III

Բայց սակաւք ի նոցանէ զմիտս հաճելով՝ ասէին զայս. «Այո, արքայ քաջ, այդ այդպէս է որպէս ասացերդ, եւ արդ կարես զամենայն ուղղութեամբ նուաճել. չիք ինչ այն որ ըստ քո կամսդ արտաքս կարէ ելանել. զի տուեալ է քեզ աստուածոցն, զի զամենայն զոր եւ կամիս՝ կարես առնել: Մի՛ նեղեալ տագնապիր յանձն քո եւ հարկաներ զմիտս մեր ամենեցուն. թերեւս եւ դիւր իցեն հնարք իրացն կատարածի: Երկայնամիտ լեր, եւ համբերութեամբ թողացո մարդկանդ անդրէն զքրիստոնէութիւն, եւ դոքաւք զստամբակսն ածցես ի հաւանութիւն»:

Հաճոյ թուեցաւ բանն առաջի թագաւորին. եւ անդէն վաղվաղակի կոչէր զառաջեաւ յամենայն ազգացն որ ունէին զքրիստոնէութիւնն, որ ի զաւրու նորա էին, եւ բռնաբար արգելեալ էր զնոսա, զի մի՛ ոք իշխան լիցի յանդիման պաշտել զԱստուած: Քանզի որ ընդդէմ կացին, չարչարեաց եւ արգել ի նոցանէ զյայտնի պաշտաւնն, եւ ոմանց ոմանց ակամայ երկիր ետ պագանել արեգական, եւ նըստոյց ի սուգ տրտմութեան զամենայն զաւրականսն:

Իսկ այն աւր հրամայէր անդրէն համարձակութեամբ ըստ առաջին կարգին հաստատուն կալ յաւրէնս քրիստոնէութեանն: Իսկ որք յանցաւորքն էին, ոչ կամէին վաղվաղակի առանց մեծի ապաշխարութեան գալ եւ խառնել

But a few of them contented themselves and said: "Yes, valiant king, that is so, and now you can rightly subdue them all. There is nothing beyond the reach of your will, for the gods have granted you the ability to do anything you wish. Do not be troubled or grieve yourself, and do not attack all our plans. Perhaps there are simple means by which to accomplish things. Be forbearing and patiently allow these men to be Christians, for in so doing you will bring the stubborn ones to your allegiance."

This speech pleased the king, who right away summoned all the Christians in his army who had been forcibly prohibited from taking the liberty to worship God in his presence. For among those who stood before him, he had punished and opposed those who held prominent positions, forced some to worship the sun, and brought lamentations to all the soldiers.

On that day he commanded them to fearlessly and as previously stand firm in Christianity, but those who had been held culpable did not resolve to immediately come and mingle

ի կարգ քրիստոնէութեան, հրամայէր թագաւորն՝ զի բռնի կալցին եւ տարցեն յեկեղեցին իւրեանց: Եւ երիցանցն համարձակէր, որպէս զիարդ եւ զիտիցեն՝ ըստ կարգին իւրեանց արասցեն: Եւ զհատեալ ռոճիկսն կարգէր անդրէն իւրաքանչիւր, եւ զարգելեալ բազմականսն ի նոցանէ՝ ի տեղի հրամայէր մատուցանել, եւ հանապազորդ յարքունիս մտանել ոչ արգելոյր զնոսա. եւ զամենայն որ զիարդ եւ կարգեալ էին յառաջագոյն՝ անդրէն յաւրինէր: Խոնարհէր եւ խաւսէր ընդ նոսա սիրով ըստ առաջին սովորութեանն:

Եւ իբրեւ զայս ամենայն արար եւ կարգեաց, յանդիման նոցա թողութեան հրովարտակս առաքէր ընդ ամենայն երկիր իշխանութեան տէրութեան իւրոյ վասն քրիստոնէից:

Եթէ ի կապանս ոք կայցէ, արքունի հրամանաւ արձակեալ լիցի. եւ եթէ ինչք ուրուք յափշտակեալ իցեն, դարձցին անդրէն: Սոյնպէս եւ երկիրք եթէ հայրենիք, եթէ պարգեւականք եւ եթէ քաղաքգինք, եւ հանեալ ուրուք իցէ, հրամայեցաք զի դարձցին:

Եւ իբրեւ այսմ ամենայնի զնոսա տեղեակս առնէր, խնդրէր ի նոցանէ վկայութիւն հաւատարմութեան յերկիրն Հայոց, եւ երդմամբ յուխտ մտանէր առաջի նոցա՝ հաստատութեամբ ամենայն մեծամեծաց իւրոց, եթէ «Ոչ ինչ յիշեցից ամենեւին զքէն վրիժուցն խնդրելոյ: Որպէս ունէիք յառաջ ճշմարտութեամբ զաւրէնս ձեր, այսուհետեւ առաւել կալարուք. բայց միայն ի ծառայութենէ մերմէ մի՛ ելանէք»:

in the Christian ranks without great repentance, so the king commanded that they be seized and taken to their churches. He allowed the priests to do as they saw fit according to their rank, reinstated each person's stipend, reinvited his table-companions among them and did not prohibit them from entering the royal court daily, and restored all things on their former basis. He humbled himself and spoke to them courteously according to former custom.

When he had done and arranged all this, he sent edicts of amnesty regarding the Christians to all the lands in his dominion.

> *Anyone in bonds shall be set free by the royal decree, and if anyone's possessions have been taken by force, they should be restored to him. Likewise with lands, whether ancestral, or gifted or purhcased with money, if they have been seized by anyone we have commanded that they be restored.*

When he had apprised them of all this, he sought from them a testimony of his faithfulness to Armenia and pronounced an oath before them in firmness with all their grandees: "I shall not at all demand revenge against you. As you formerly followed your religion truthfully, from now on hold to it more; only do not withdraw from our service."

Զայս ամենայն գրէր եւ ցուցանէր յերկիրն Հայոց եւ ի բազում յայլ աշխարհս, որ ունէին զաւրէնս քրիստոնէութեան. եւ ինքն գաղտ խորամանկեալ փութացեալ դեսպանս առաքէր առ Մարկիանոս կայսր: Եւ իբրեւ ստուգեալ ճշմարտեաց, եթէ Հոռոմք ի բաց կացին ձեռնտու լինել քրիստոնէութեանն ոչ զաւրու աւգնականութեամբ եւ ոչ այլ իրաւք, դարձեալ անդրէն ի նոյն յառաջին կարծիս մոլորութեանն շրջեցաւ: Զի զյաջողութիւն իրացն ի ձեռն իւրոց պաշտաւնէիցն հրամայէր. եւ այնպէս ածէր զմտաւ, եթէ ըստ առաջին կարծեացն կատարեսցեն զամենայն:

Իսկ Հայք թէպէտ եւ ընկալան զգիրն խաբեբայ ողոքանաց թագաւորին, որ ի վերոյ ունէր զաւետիս կենաց եւ ի ներքոյ զդառնութիւն մահու, զարմացեալ ընդ թերի խորհուրդսն՝ ասէին ցմիմեանս. «Քանի՜ լիրբ է խորամանկ խաբէութիւն նորա, զի երկիցս եւ երիցս զփորձ առեալ կըշտամբեցաւ եւ ոչ ամաչէ: Եւ տեղեակ եղեալ մերոյ անքակ միաբանութեանս, տակաւին լրբի եւ լկնի. զհետ մտեալ՝ կամի զմեզ լքուցանել:

«Իսկ հաւատացո՞ւք անհաստատ հրամանի նորա. զո՞ր բարեգործութիւն տեսաք առ ամենայն եկեղեցիս, որ են յաշխարհին Պարսից: Զի որ ինքն իւր չար է, այլում բարի ոչ կարէ լինել. եւ որ ինքն ընդ խաւար գնայ, այլում ոչ առաջնորդէ ճշմարտութեան լուսով: Որպէս զի չիք յանիրաւութենէ արդարութիւն, այսպէս եւ ոչ ի ստութենէ ճշմարտութիւն, սոյնպէս եւ ի խռովասէր մտաց՝ ակնկալութիւն խաղաղութեան:

All this he wrote and indicated to Armenia and to many other countries that held to the Christian religion; and with secret deceit he swiftly sent envoys to the emperor Marcian. But when he confirmed that the Romans had withdrawn their help from the Christians, with troops and by other means, he reverted to his former erroneous views. He attributed the success of their affairs to his ministers, and thus thought that they could accomplish everything according to his former ideas.

When the Armenians received the deceitful and flattering letter of the king, which on its surface had the promise of life and beneath had the bitterness of death, they were surprised by its defective counsel, and said one to the other: "How shameless is his crafty deceit, for two and three times he tried and was reproved without shame. He is aware of our indissoluble union, yet he is brazen and impudent—pursuing us, he wants to weaken us.

"Should we believe his fickle command? What benevolence have we seen toward all the churches in the empire of the Persians? He who is himself evil can do no goodness to others; he who walks in the darkness cannot lead others by the light of truth. As justice cannot come from injustice, nor truth from falsehood, so neither from a disturbed mind can there be expectation of peace.

CHAPTER III

«Այլ մեք ապրեալքս զաւրութեամբն Աստուծոյ, եւ հաստատեալք հաւատովքն ի յոյսն Քրիստոսի, որ եկն եւ էառ ի սուրբ կուսէն զմարմին մերոյ բնութեանս, եւ միացեալ անբաժանելի աստուածութեամբն՝ ընկալաւ զչարչարանս մերոյ մեղաց ի յիւր մարմինն, եւ նովին խաչեցաւ եւ թաղեցաւ եւ յարուցեալ երեւեցաւ բազմաց, եւ վերացաւ յանդիման աշակերտացն առ Հայր իւր, եւ նստաւ ընդ աջմէ զաւրութեանն, զսոյն հաւատամք Աստուած ճշմարիտ, եւ նմին ակն ունիմք, որ փառաւք Հաւր եւ զաւրութեամբ գայ յարուցանել զամենայն ննջեցեալս, եւ նորոգել զհնութիւն արարածոց, առնել համառաւտս յաւիտենից ի մէջ արդարոց եւ մեղաւորաց:

«Ոչ պատրիմք իբրեւ զտղայս, եւ ոչ մոլորիմք իբրեւ զանտեղեակս, եւ ոչ խաբիմք իբրեւ զտգէտս, այլ պատրաստ եմք ամենայն փորձութեանց: Եւ աղաչեմք զԱստուած, եւ անդադար խնդրեմք ի բազում ողորմութենէ նորա, զի յորում սկսաք՝ ի նմին եւ կատարեսցուք քաջութեամբ, եւ ոչ վատութեամբ: Զի արդ արեւելք եւ արեւմուտք գիտացին զձեր աստուածամարտդ լինել, եւ զմեզի զուր սպանանել ի վերայ ամենայն վաստակոցն մերոց: Վկայեն մեզ երկինք երկնաւորաւք եւ երկիր երկրաւորաւք, եթէ չեմք ինչ մեղուցեալ ի միտս մեր անգամ. եւ ի վերայ պարգեւաց եւ բարիս առնելոյ մեզ՝ զճշմարիտ կեանս կամիք հանել ի մէնջ, որում չիք հնար, եւ այլ մի՛ լիցի:

"But we are delivered by the power of God and with firm belief in the hope of Christ, Who became embodied in our nature through the Holy Virgin, united with His indivisible godhead, bore the torment of our sins upon his body, and with the same body was crucified and buried, and having arisen appeared to many and ascended before His apostles to His Father, and sat at the right hand of the power, and we believe Him to be the same as the true God, and we wait for Him to come with the glory and power of the Father to raise all who are dead, and to renew His old creatures, and to make an eternal judgment upon the just and unjust.

"We will not stumble like children, nor err like the unlearned, nor be deceived like the ignorant, but are ready for all temptations. And we pray to God, and unceasingly seek His abundant mercy, that whatever we have started, we may also complete with courage and not cowardice. For East and West have understood that you fight against God, and have killed us in vain despite all our service. Heaven and its beings earth and its beings are our witnesses that not even in our minds are we at fault; yet instead of [granting] rewards and doing good to us, you resolve to take true life from us, which is not possible and shall not come to pass.

«Իսկ արդ հաւատացո՞ւք անարժան բերանոյ նորա, որ ստիպէր չարաչար յուրացութիւն, եւ այսաւր առանց մի ինչ բարիս գործելոյ լինիցի՞ նա քարոզիչ աւետեաց: Եւ որ հայհոյէրն զՔրիստոս, եւ ուրացուցանէր ի նմանէ զհաւատացեալս, այսաւր ակամայ խոստովանութեանն ոչ կարեմք վաղվաղակի յանձն առնուլ: Եւ որ երդնոյրն ի սնոտի պաշտամունս իւրոյ մոլորութեանն՝ անցուցանել զամենայն չարչարանս ընդ պաշտաւնեայս եկեղեցւոյ, արդ եկեալ գողանալով զհնութիւն մատուցանէ, եւ այնու կամի զամենայն չարութիւն իւր ի մեզ հեղուլ: Ոչ այդմ հաւատամք, եւ ոչ զսուտ հրամանդ յանձն առնումք»:

Իսկ նա իբրեւ գիտաց, եթէ ոչ կարեմ քակել զհաստատութիւն միաբանելոցն, յայնժամ քակեաց յինքենէ զծերն լի դառնութեամբ, յորում հանգուցեալ էր սատանայ զաւրութեամբ իւրով, եւ բազում գործեալ էր նորա նախճիրս. որոյ կերակուր կամաց իւրոց էր ի մանկութենէ անարատ մարմին սրբոց, եւ ըմպելի անյագութեան նորին՝ արիւն անմեղացն: Յաւելոյր եւս ի վերայ չարութեան նորա եւ զիր մահաբեր հրամանն. գունդս գունդս յամենայն աշխարհացն գումարէր ընդ նմա, եւ բազում երամակս փղաց յղէր ընդ նմա:

Հասեալ մերձ ի սահմանս Հայոց՝ մտանէր ի քաղաքն Փայտակարան, եւ զզաւրսն ամենայն սփռէր տարածանէր շուրջ զքաղաքաւն առ ի զգուշութիւն պատրաստութեան իւրոյ չարահնար խորհրդոցն: Եւ յամուր որջն մտեալ հին վիշապն չարաթոյն, եւ բազում կեղծաւորութեամբ զխնքն թաքուցանելով յաներկիւղութիւն, հեռաւորացն ահագին ձայնիւ սաստէր. եւ ի մերձաւորսն իբրեւ զաւձ սողալով փչէր: Սա էր իշխան եւ հրամանատար ամենայն տէրութեանն Պարսից, որում անուն էր Միհրներսեհ, եւ չէր ոք ամենեւին, որ իշխէր ըստ ձեռն նորա ելանել: Եւ ոչ միայն մեծամեծք եւ փոքունք, այլ եւ ինքն թագաւորն հրամանի նորա անսայր. որոյ եւ ձախող իրացն իսկ բուռն հարեալ էր նորա:

"Are we now to believe his unworthy mouth that forces grievous apostacy? And without having effected any good, will he now preach good promises? We cannot immediately believe this unwilling avowal of a man who blasphemed Christ and apostatized his believers, who swore in his vain and aberrant cult and brought to pass all torments upon the ministers of the church and has now come to offer duplicitous thanks with which he resolves to pour out all his evil upon us. We neither believe him nor accept his false command."

When the king understood that he could not disband their firm brotherhood, he bitterly released the old man [Mihr Narseh] whom Satan had lodged with his power, and who effected much carnage; whose preferred food from childhood was the immaculate flesh of the saints, and whose insatiable drink was the blood of the innocents. Upon this evil he added his own deadly command: He gathered legion upon legion [of the Persian army] from throughout all the land and sent many contingents of elephants with them.

He came upon the borders of Armenia, entered the city of Paytakaran, and distributed his army around the city in careful preparation [to effect] his wicked design. The old poisonous dragon entered his secure lair, hiding himself with great hypocrisy so as not to be feared, and he rebuked those who were faraway with his formidable voice, and those who were nearby by slithering and hissing like a snake. This was the prince and commander of the whole empire of the Persians, whose name was Mihr Narseh, from whose clutches no one at all could escape. Not only did great and small obey his command, but so did the king himself, whom he had caught with his sinister devices.

Դ

ՎԱՍՆ ԵՐԿՊԱՌԱԿՈՒԹԵԱՆ ԻՇԽԱՆԻՆ ՍԻՒՆԵԱՑ ԵՒ ԸՆԿԵՐԱՑ ԻՒՐՈՑ

Մինչեւ ցայս վայր ոչ ինչ կարի զանգիտէի պատմել զհարուածս ազգիս մերոյ, որ յարտաքին թշնամեացն ճշմարտութեան չարաչար յարեան ի վերայ մեր. որք սակաւագոյնք հարին զմեզ, եւ յոլովագոյնք հարեալ գտան ի մէնջ, քանզի դեռեւս միաբանք եւ հաւասարք էաք: Թէպէտ եւ ոմանք ի ծածուկ ունէին զերկմտութիւն նենգութեանն, սակայն յաչս արտաքնոցն ահաւոր երեւէր միաբանութիւնն. որպէս յերկուս եւ յերիս տեղիս ոչ կարացին կալ առաջի:

Արդ յայսմ հետէ եւ անդր, ուր սպրդեալ անկանի երկպառակութիւն ի ներքս, ընդ քակել միաբանութեանն՝ եւ երկնաւոր առաքինութիւնն հեռանայ. եւ անձնընտիրք լինելով՝ յոյժ բազմանայ լալումն ողբոյս: Քանզի հատեալ անկեալ անդամքն, որ յառաջագոյն սորուն սուրբ մարմնոյս էին, դառնայ մարդ յարտաասուս առաջի մերձակայ դիականն. եւս առաւել լնու դառնութեամբ ի վերայ այնորիկ, որ յոգի եւ ի մարմին առ հասարակ դիակնանայ: Եւ եթէ ի վերայ միոյ անձին այսպէս, ո՞րչափ եւս առաւել ի վերայ ողջոյն ազգի միոջ:

IV

ON THE DISSENT OF THE PRINCE OF SYUNIK AND HIS FRIENDS

Until now, I have not hesitated to explain the blows that the foreign enemies of the truth maliciously inflicted upon us, a few of whom struck us and found many struck by us, for we were still united as equals. Although some [of us] were covertly and deceitfully of two minds, suddenly our brotherhood appeared fearsome in the eyes of the foreigners, such that they could not find solid ground from which to oppose us.

Henceforth, where dissension creeps in, our brotherhood shall dissolve, and with it, heavenly virtue; then we shall grow self-centered and our cries of lamentation shall multiply. For when those members who previously belonged to the holy body are cut loose, their fellow men turn to tears before their corpses, and become filled with even more bitterness upon those who become corpses in both soul and body. And if it is so for individuals, how much more for the life of an entire nation!

Այլ յայսմ տեղւոջ ոչ միայն ի վերայ միոյ ազգի է ողբումնս մեր, այլ ի վերայ ազգաց եւ աշխարհաց. զոր եւ յառաջ մատուցեալ ասացից ըստ կարգի, թէպէտ եւ ոչ խնդութեան մտաւք: Ահա ակամայ ճառագրեմ զբազումս որպէս կորեան ոմանք ի ճշմարիտ կենացն իւրեանց, եւ պատճառք եղեն բազմաց կորստեանն, ոմանց՝ երեւելեացս միայն, եւ այլոց երեւելեաց եւ աներեւութից: Եւ այն՝ եւս չար է քան զամենայն. դուռն՝ զոր բացին կորստեան, Աստուծո՛յ միայն կարողութիւն է փակել զնա. այլ ըստ մարդկան սահման՝ ահա անցեալ է հնար:

Այս անաւրէն Միհրներսեհ, քանզի յառաջագոյն ստուգեալ գիտէր զամբարշտութիւնն Վասակայ, եւ յայնմ ժամանակի եւս յղէր եւ կոչէր զնա առինքն: Որպէս նորա իսկ յառաջագոյն զատեալ եւ որոշեալ էր ի միաբանութենէն Հայոց, եկն եւ յանդիման եղեւ. եւ ստուգէր զիւր հաւատարմութիւնն եւ զՀայոց անիրաւ ապստամբութիւնն: Ցաւել եւ պատմեաց եւս առաւելաբանութեամբ զոր ինչ ոչ էր գործեալ Հայոց, եւ կամէր ընտանեբար ընդ միտ մտանել անաւրինին:

Բայց նա թէպէտ եւ ի ներքոյ յոյժ դարովէր զնա, այլ արտաքին դիմաւք մեծարեաց, եւ եդ առաջի նորա զմեծամեծ պարգեւս երկրաւորս: Եւ խոստացաւ նմա իշխանութիւն աւելի քան զոր ունէրն, եւ հայեցոյց զնա ի կարծիս սնոտիս, որ ի վեր էր քան զիւր տէրութիւնն. իբր թէ անկ իցէ նմա հասանել մինչ ի թագաւորական վիճակն. բայց միայն հնարս իրացն խնդրեսցէ, թէ որպէս քակտեսցի միաբանութիւն ուխտին Հայոց, եւ թագաւորին կամքն կատարեսցին յաշխարհին:

But here our lamentation does not only resound for one nation, but for numerous nations and countries, which I will tell of in order, albeit without joy of mind. Unwillingly do I describe these many cases—how some of them lost their own true lives and became the cause for the loss of lives of many others (visible in some cases, and both visible and invisible in others). The worst of all is that they opened the gate to destruction that only God can close, for to do so lies beyond the capability of man.

This lawless Mihr Narseh sent and called for Vasak, knowing beforehand of his impiety. Vasak, who had already separated himself from the Armenian brotherhood, came to Mihr Narseh, confirmed his fidelity and assured him of the disloyal Armenian revolt. He exaggerated and overstated what the Armenians had done and resolved to amicably influence the mind of the lawless one.

But although [Mihr Narseh] inwardly reviled [Vasak], he outwardly honored him, conferred great material gifts upon him, promised him greater authority than what he possessed, and turned his attention to the vain expectation of attaining higher authority, as though he might become king if only he could find a way to dissolve the brotherhood of the Armenian faithful and effect the will of the king in that land.

CHAPTER IV

Եւ իբրեւ յանձն էառ զամենայն ինչ՝ երթալ զկնի կամաց նորա, գիտաց եւ ծերն դառնացեալ, եթէ թմբրեալ եւ ցնորեալ եւ քակեալ է ի հաստատութենէ միաբանելոցն. յոյժ մխիթարեցաւ ի միտս իւր տրտմեալս, եւ էած զմտաւ՝ թէ եւ զամենեսեան այսպէս կարիցեմ որսալ յանգիւտ կորուստն: Եւ իւրոյ հնարագիտութեանն տայր զիմաստութիւնն. եւ այնմ ոչ էր տեղեակ, թէ նա իւրով ի զիւր անձն զատեալ եւ որոշեալ է ի սուրբ եկեղեցւոյն, հեռացեալ եւ աստարացեալ ի սիրոյն Քրիստոսի:

Քանզի մոռացաւնք եղեն նմա գալուստ Որդւոյն Աստուծոյ, եւ ոչ յիշեաց զքարոզութիւն սուրբ աւետարանին. եւ ոչ ի սպառնալեացն զանգիտեաց, եւ ոչ յաւետիսն մխիթարեցաւ: Ուրացաւ զաւազանն՝ որ յղացաւ զնա, եւ ոչ յիշեաց զընկալուչ սուրբ հոգին՝ որ ծնաւ զնա: Անարգեաց զմարմինն պատուական՝ սրով սրբեցաւն, եւ առ ոտն եհար զարիւնն կենդանի՝ որով եւ քաւեցաւն ի մեղաց: Ջնջեաց զգիր որդէգրութեանն, եւ իւրովք ձեռաւք խորտակեաց զհաստատուն կնիք մատանւոյն: Ել ի թուոյ երանելեացն, եւ ապստամբեցոյց ընդ իւր զբազումս:

Ձեռն էարկ կամակորութեամբ եւ եմուտ յորդէգրութիւն դիւապաշտութեանն, եւ եղեւ աման չարին, եւ ելից զնա սատանայ ամենայն խորամանկութեամբ: Ի ձեռն էառ իբրեւ զվահան, եւ ագաւ զնա իբրեւ զզրահս, եւ եղեւ իբր զինուոր կատարեալ կամաց նորա: Մարտեաւ հնարիւք ընդ իմաստունս, եւ յոյժ խորագիտութեամբ ընդ գիտունս, յայտնի ընդ անմեղս, եւ ի ծածուկ ընդ խորհրդականս. ձեռն էարկ եւ եհան զբազումս ի գնդէն Քրիստոսի, եւ խառնեաց ի գունդս դիւաց: Եւ ի բազում յայլ տեղիս գողաբար սողեցաւ եւ եմուտ իբրեւ զաւձ ի մէջ ամրացելոցն. եւ խրամ հատեալ յափշտակեաց եւ էառ եւ եհան յայտնութեամբ զբազումս յազատաց եւ զբազմագոյնս ի շինականաց, եւ զայլ ոմանս յանուանեալ քահանայից:

When [Vasak] consented to do everything according to [Mihr Narseh's] will, the bitter old man understood that Vasak was wearied and vexed and had detached from the firm brotherhood. He was very much consoled in his sorrowful mind, believing that he might succeed at last in luring them into boundless destruction. He attributed his machinations to his wisdom, not realizing that [Vasak] himself had separated from the holy church and estranged himself from the love of Christ.

For he had forgotten about the coming of the Son of God and no longer recalled the preaching of the Holy Gospel. He no longer feared threats or found comfort in the Gospel. He denied the [baptismal] font that conceived him and did not recall reception of the Holy Spirit that had begotten him. He brought into contempt the honorable body, with which he was made holy, and trod upon the living blood, by which he received penance for his sins. He blotted out the letter of adoption and with his own hand broke the firm seal off of his ring. He then left the number of the blessed ones and drew many people after him.

He crookedly undertook to worship demons and became a vessel of evil, and Satan filled him with every cunning, taking him as a shield and wearing him as armor, so that he became like a soldier fulfilling [Satan's] will. He fought with artifice against the wise and with cunning against the knowledgeable; openly against the innocent and secretly against the discreet; he drove many from the army of Christ, and mingled them with the hosts of demons. He slithered thief-like into many other places and entered the strongholds; and breaking in, he seized and openly removed many of the nobles and peasants, and others called priests.

Որոց անունքն են այս՝ գործակցաց նորա.

Իշխանն Ռշտունեաց՝ Արտակ անուն:

Իշխանն Խորխոռունեաց՝ Գադիշոյ անուն:

Իշխանն Վահեւունեաց՝ Գիւտ անուն:

Իշխանն Բագրատունեաց՝ Տիրոց անուն:

Իշխանն Ապահունեաց՝ Մանէճ անուն:

Իշխանն Գաբեղէնից՝ Արտէն անուն:

Իշխանն Ակէոյ՝ Ընջուղ անուն:

Իշխանն Ուրծայ՝ Ներսեհ անուն:

Իշխանն մեւս եւս Պալունեաց՝ Վարազշապուհ անուն:

Սեպուհ մի Ամատունեաց Մանէն անուն:

Բազում եւ այլ ազատ մարդիկ, զոր ոստանիկսն անուանեն՝ յարքունի տանէ:

Եւ բովանդակ զիւր բոլոր աշխարհն ապստամբեցոյց յուրացութիւն, ոչ միայն ըստ աշխարհական բազմութեանն, այլ եւ զբազումս ի սուրբ ուխտէ եկեղեցւոյն. մանաւանդ սուտ երիցամբքն ՝ որով գործէր զչարիսն. երէց մի Զանգակ անուն, երէց մի Պետրոս անուն, սարկաւագ մի Սահակ անուն, սարկաւագ մի Մուշի անուն, զորս յղէր առ անմեղ մարդիկ, խաբէր եւ պատրէր. սուրբ աւետարանաւն երդնուին եւ ասէին, եթէ «Ի թագաւորէն շնորհեցի ամենեցունց քրիստոնէութիւնդ»: Եւ այսպէս խորամանկ խաբեութեամբ հանէին զբազումս ի սուրբ միաբանութենէն, ածէին եւ խառնէին ի գունդս ուրացողացն:

These are the names of his associates:

The prince of Reshtunik, Artak.

The prince of Khorkhorrunik, Gadisho.

The prince of Vahevunik, Giwt.

The prince of Bagratunik, Tirots.

The prince of Apahunik, Manej.

The prince of Gabeghiank, Arten.

The prince of Ake, Enjugh.

The prince of Urts, Nerseh.

Another prince of the Balunik, Varazshapuh.

A sepuh of the Amatunik, Manen.

And many others azats, whom they call *ostanik*, [which means] from the royal house.

He drew the entire land into apostasy—not only the masses, but also the holy clergy of the church, and especially the false priests through whom he worked malice: a priest named Zangak, a priest named Petros, a deacon named Sahak, and a deacon named Mushi, whom he sent to innocent men to deceive. They swore on the Holy Gospel, and said: "Christianity shall be granted to all by the king." And thus, by this artifice, they detached many from the holy brotherhood, bringing and mingling them among the hosts of the apostates.

Եւ ժողովեաց զամենայն գայթակղութիւն, եւ արար գունդ զաւրաց բազմաց. գրեաց եւ եցոյց զբազումս ի նոցանէ յականէ յանուանէ մեծ հազարապետին, եւ զիւր քաջութիւն արութեանն, մեծապէս պարծելով՝ ո՛րպէս աշակերտեաց ի մոլորութիւն խաբէութեան, եւ բաժանեալս եւ երկցեղս երեւեցոյց զզաւրսն Հայոց:

Եւ իբրեւ այս ամենայն չարիք յաջողեցան նմա, քակեաց եւ զմիաբանութիւն աշխարհին Վրաց ի Հայոց, եւ Աղուանիցն ոչ ետ յառաջ խաղալ. եւ զաշխարհն Աղձնեաց ըստ նմին իսկ աւրինակի յետս կալաւ: Գրեաց հրովարտակ եւ աշխարհին Յունաց, ցուցանելով նոցա այլ ընդ այլոյ ստութեամբ, առ այր մի, որոյ Վասակ անուն էր, յայնց Մամիկոնենից՝ որ կան ի ծառայութեան Յունաց: Եւ ի թըշուառութեան ժամանակին այրն այն սպարապետ էր Ստորին Հայոց, եւ հաւատարիմ զաւրացն Հոռոմց ի սահմանին Պարսից, եւ արտաքոյ էր աւրինացն Աստուծոյ գործովք իւրովք: Եգիտ այս Վասակ զայն Վասակ իւր գործակից ի մեծամեծ չարիսն՝ զոր միաբանեցին երկոքեանն:

Գրէր նա եւ ցուցանէր հանապազորդ, իբր թէ ամենայն Հայք զկնի իւր միաբանեցին: Եւ զնոյն գիր մեծաւ զգուշութեամբ ներքին Վասակն տայր տանել ի թագաւորանիստ քաղաքն կայսեր. մինչեւ զսուրբ եպիսկոպոսացն զմիտս եւս ուծացոյց ի նոցանէ, եւ զամենայն զաւրսն Յունաց յերկբայս արար յուխտէն:

He assembled all those whom he had tempted and formed a large, armed force; he wrote many of their names one by one and presented them to the great hazarbed [Mihr Narseh], and greatly boasting of his strength and valor, he taught them to aberrate and to deceive, and gave the appearance that the Armenian army had been split in two.

And when he had succeeded in all this evildoing, he dissolved the brotherhood between the Georgians and Armenians and did not allow either the Aghuans or Aghdznis to advance. He wrote a letter full of equivocations to the Greeks, to a man named Vasak from the Mamikonian clan, who are in service to the Greeks. In this time of misery, that man was the sparapet of Lower Armenia, loyal to the Roman army at the Iranian border and without the divine law in his workings. This Vasak found in the other Vasak an associate for effecting great misery, in which they united together.

He wrote and continually gave the appearance that all Armenians were united with him. And this same letter Vasak carefully and covertly had delivered to the royal capital, and so much as distanced the minds of the holy bishops from them [the Armenians] and put doubt in the minds of the entire Greek army about their covenant.

Մանաւանդ զի ի ձեռն սուտ քահանայիցն պատրէր եւ խաբէր իբրեւ ճշմարիտ մարդովք. աւետարան հանդերձ խաչիւ տայր տանել, եւ զիւր զամենայն սատանայական ստութիւնն նոքաւք ծածկէր: Դնէր զինքն յաստուածպաշտութեան կարգի եւ զամենայն կողմ ուրացելոցն. առաւել զինքն հաւաստէր հաստատուն քան զամենայն զաւրսն Հայոց. երդնոյր եւ հաստատէր, եւս եւ զամենայն հրամանս թողութեան յարքունուստ ցուցանէր:

Այն էին եւ կամք Յունաց աշխարհին, լսել զայն ախորժութեամբ. այլ ի ձեռն նորա առաւել եւս ի նոյն յեղեալ տապալեցան:

Սոյնպէս առնէր եւ ընդ ամենայն կողմանս ամրականաց աշխարհին, ի Տմորիսն եւ ի Կորդիսն, յԱրցախ եւ յԱղուանսն, ի Վիրս եւ յաշխարհն Խաղտեաց. յղէր պնդէր, զի ապնջականութեան որք արժանի մի՛ արասցէ:

Եւ ըստ մեծի չարութեան նորա առաւել եւս ժամանակն եբեր նմա զյաջողութիւն իրացն. զի ամենեւին արտաքուստ աւգնական որք ոչ գտաւ գնդին Հայոց, բաց յայնց Հոնաց, որոց բանս եդեալ էր: Սակայն եւ վասն նոցա կուտեաց զբազում այրուձին Արեաց, արգել եւ փակեաց զդրրունս ելին նոցա: Քանզի ոչ տայր դադար ամենեւին թագաւորին Պարսից, այլ յղէր եւ կոչէր գունդս բազումս ի պահակն Ճորայ, եւ զՎրաց աշխարհն բովանդակ անդ գումարէր, զզաւրսն Լփնաց եւ զՃղբաց, եւ զՎատոն, զԳաւն եւ զԳղուարն եւ զԽրսանն եւ զՀեճմատակն, զՓասխն եւ զՓոսխն, եւ զՓիւքուան եւ զամենայն զաւրսն Թաւասպարանն, զլեռնայինն եւ զդաշտայինն, եւ զամենայն ամրակողմըն լերանցն: Էր զոր կարասեաւ, մեծաւ պարգեւաւք եւ առատաձեռն բաշխելով զգանձսն արքունի, եւ էր զոր հրամանաւ թագաւորին սաստիւ տագնապէր:

Above all he separated them by means of the false priests who concealed all his Satanic lies while bearing the Gospel and cross. He insinuated himself in the ranks of the godly, surrounding himself with apostates; thus, he believed himself to wield more power than the entire Armenian army. He swore and gave assurances and showed all commands of remission to be from the court.

The Greeks shared the same will, so they listened to this agreeably; and because of Vasak they became more removed [from the Armenians].

He acted in the same manner with all the strongholds of the land, in Tmorik, Korduk, Artsakh, Aghuank, Georgia and Khaghtik, he sent [people] to insist that they not receive [the Armenians] hospitably.

And by his great wickedness, time brought him yet more success, for the Armenian army was entirely deprived of foreign and external aid, with the exception of the Huns, with whom they had an agreement. Yet because of [the Armenians], he gathered the large cavalry of the Aryans and blocked their gates of passage. For he did not give the king of the Persians any rest, but sent and summoned a great military unit to the gate of Chor and gathered all [the forces] of the Georgians, the forces of the Lpink and Chighbk, Vatk, Gavk and Ghuark and Khrsank and Hechmatak, Paskh, Poskh, Pyukuan, and the entire army of Tavasparank, from the highlands and the lowlands, and all the mountain strongholds. Some [he captured] with possessions, great gifts and the distribution of abundant royal treasures, and others he pressed by the threat of the king's command.

CHAPTER IV

Զայս ամենայն իբրեւ արար եւ կատարեաց ըստ հրամանի թագաւորին, աւր ըստ աւրէ գրէր եւ ցուցանէր մեծ հազարապետին Պարսից, որ դաւղեալ եւ թաքուցեալ էր ի քաղաքն Փայտակարան: Համարձակեցաւ այնուհետեւ եւ նա ցուցանել զինքն բազում ազգաց, էր՝ որոց ահ արկանէր, եւ էր՝ որոց սիրով պարգեւս բաշխէր: Կոչէր առ ինքն զՎասակ, եւ որք ընդ նմա իշխանքն ամենեքեան, բազում պարգեւս շնորհէր նոցա յարքունուստ, եւ զաւրացն՝ որ ի նորա բանի էին: Տանէր զառաջեաւ եւ զուրացեալ երիցունսն. ցուցանէր, հաստատէր եւ յայտ առնէր, եթէ սոքաւք որսացայց զնոսա՝ քակտել ի միաբան ուխտէն: Իսկ հազարապետն իբրեւ զայն լսէր՝ յոյժ շնորհակալ լինէր երկոցունցն, եւ յոյս առաջի դնէր նոցա. «Եթէ լիցի մեր յաղթութիւն, զայլոց քահանայից կեանս դոցա շնորհեցից, եւ զմեծ վաստակ դոցա ցուցից թագաւորին»:

Եւ այսպէս շարժեաց եւ շփոթեաց զաշխարհն Հայոց, մինչեւ զբազում եղբարս հարազատս քակեաց ի միմեանց, ոչ եթող միաբան զհայր եւ զորդի, եւ ի մէջ խաղաղութեան արար խռովութիւն:

Եւ անդէն իսկ յիւրում աշխարհին եղբաւրորդիք երկու էին նորա ի սուրբ ուխտին առաքինութեան. գրեաց եւ եցոյց վասն նոցա յարքունիս, եւ էառ իշխանութիւն ի վերայ կենաց նոցա, մերժեաց եւ եհան զնոսա յաշխարհէն, զի մի՛ այլ դարձցին անդրէն: Հալածեաց եւ փախոյց զամենայն միայնակեաց սաշխարհին, ոյք հայհոյէին զանդարձ ամբարշտութիւն նորա: Արար եւ կատարեաց զամենայն չարիսն ընդդէմ ճշմարտութեանն. եւ զոր ինչ ոչ գիտէին անաւրէն հեթանոսքն՝ իմացուցանէր նոցա, եւ վասն ուխտին քրիստոնէութեան, եթէ որպէս հնարիւք կարասցէ բառնալ յաշխարհէն Հայոց:

When he effected and accomplished all of this according to the king's command, he daily wrote to the great hazarbed of the Persians [Mihr Narseh], who was hiding in the city of Paytarakan. Thereafter, he went boldly and approached many nations, filling some with terror and gladly distributing gifts among others. He called for Vasak and all the princes who were with him, bestowed many gifts upon them from the court, as well as to the soldiers in agreement with him. [Vasak] took before him the apostate priests, showing and explaining how with these he would lure the others and disband them from their covenant. When the hazarbed heard this, he was very thankful to the priests and placed hope before them: "If we succeed, the possessions of the other priests shall be bestowed to you and your great services will be represented to the king."

Thus he shook and disturbed the land of Armenians, so much as estranging brothers from each other, separating son from father, and caused disturbance amid peace.

Even in his own land, where he had two nephews[41] who were among the virtuous brotherhood, he tattled on them to the royal court, received authority over their possessions and exiled them from the land so that they could not return. He persecuted and put to flight all the hermits of the land who cursed his irredeemable impiety. He effected all this evil against the truth, and imparted knowledge to the ungodly heathens, including about the Christian faithful, as to the means by which they may be severed from Armenia.

41 *nephews:* brother's sons.

CHAPTER IV

Զայս ամենայն չարիս իբրեւ ետես ի նմա Միհրներսեհ, քան յանձն իւր՝ առաւել ի նա էր յուսացեալ: Հարցանէր եւ ստուգէր՝ թէ քանի՞ այր կայ ի Հայոց աշխարհին ի գնդին Վարդանայ ընդ ամենայն բազմութիւնն: Իբրեւ լուաւ ի նըմանէ՝ թէ աւելի քան զվաթսուն հազար են, խնդրէր եւս տեղեկութիւն վասն իւրաքանչիւր անձին քաջութեան, եւ կամ քանի՛ այն ոք իցեն՝ որ սպառազէնքն իցեն, եւ կամ քանի՛ այն ոք իցեն՝ որ մերկ առանց զինու աղեղնաւորք իցեն. սոյնպէս եւ վասն վահանաւոր հետեւակացն:

Եւ իբրեւ լուաւ զթիւ համարոյ բազմութեանն, առաւել եւս փութացաւ ուսանել՝ թէ քանի՛ք իցեն պարագլուխք քաջ նահատակացն, զի երիս ընդ միոյ պատրաստեսցէ առ մի մի ի նոցանէ, թող զայլն ամենայն: Այլ եւ դրաւշից անգամ իւրաքանչիւրոց տեղեկանայր ի նմանէ. եւ թէ քանի՛ գունդ զզաւրսն բաժանիցեն, եւ ո՛ր ոք ի նոցանէ սաղարք լինիցին, եւ ո՛ր զաւրագլուխ յորմէ կողմանէ յառաջ մտանիցէ, եւ զինչ անուանք իւրաքանչիւր համհարզացն իցեն, եւ քանի՛ փողահարք ի մէջ գնդին ձայնիցեն: Ղակի՞շ գործիցեն արդեւք, եթէ արձակ բանակեսցին. ճակատ առ ճակա՞տ գործիցեն, եթէ համագունդ ընդ մի տեղի դրդիցեն: Ո՛ ոք ի նոցանէ երկբայս կայցէ, եւ կամ ո՛ ոք ի նոցանէ զանձն ի մահ դնելով գուն գործիցէ:

When Mihr Narseh saw all this evil associated with Vasak, he put more hope in him than in himself. He examined the number of men throughout Armenia under the command of Vartan. When he heard that they amounted to more than 60,000, he required additional information as to the strengths of each, the number of those who were armed, the number of unarmed archers, and likewise concerning the shielded infantry.

Then, on hearing all this, [Mihr Narseh] became more eager to learn about how many men would be leading the valiant warriors, so as to outnumber them three-to-one (let alone the others). He also inquired concerning each banner, as to how many regiments the army was divided into, who among them were officers, which commander would lead the battle on which side, the names of each adjutant, and how many trumpeters would sound in the army. Would they cast up entrenchments or encamp openly? Would they do battle head-to-head[42] or concentrate them all together on one spot? Who among them would waver, and who among them would fight to the death?

42 *Head-to-head:* along the battlefront.

Եւ իբրեւ զայս ամենայն տեղեկացաւ ի նմանէ, կոչէր զամենայն զաւրագլխեանն, պատուէր հրամանի տայր ամենեցուն յանդիման նորա, զի խրատու նորա լուիցեն ամենեքեան: Եւ զամենայն զաւրսն զաւրագլխաւքն հանդերձ յանձն առնէր առն միում յաւագացն, որում անուն էր Մուշկան Նիւսալաւուրտ:

Եւ ինքն խաղայր անդէն գնայր յերկիրն Արեւելից. եւ յանդիման եղեալ մեծի թագաւորին, պատմէր զամենայն անցս իրացն, զիւր հնարաւոր իմաստութիւնն եւ զՎասակայ խաբեբայ պատրանս հայթայթանացն. ո՛րպէս զառաջինն զիւր զամբարշտութիւնն կամեցաւ ծածկել այնու՝ զի քակեալ երկպառակեաց զգունդն Հայոց:

Իբրեւ լուաւ զայս ամենայն թագաւորն ի բերանոյ մեծ հազարապետին, դառնացաւ յանձն իւր, եւ ասէ անսուտ երդմամբ. «Եթէ ապրեսցի անաւրէնն այնի մեծ պատերազմէն, մեծաւ անարգանաւք տամ ըմպել նմա զբաժակն դառնութեան մահու»:

When [Mihr Narseh] had been informed on all these points, he summoned all of his commanders and ordered them all, in [Vasak's] presence, to heed his instructions. Then he committed the entire army and all the commanders to one member of senior rank, whose name was Mushkan Niwsalavurt.

He himself set forth toward the land of the East and appeared before the great king, to whom he related all the occurrences which had taken place, including his devious intelligence and Vasak's deceptive flattery to procure his ends, and how he had at first resolved to conceal his impiety to dissolve and divide the Armenian forces.

Now when the king heard all this from the mouth of the great hazarbed, he became embittered within, and swore this inviolable oath: "If that renegade survives that great battle, with great dishonor will I have him drink from the bitter cup of death."

INDEX

INDEX

SOPHENE

CPSIA information can be obtained
at www.ICGtesting.com
Printed in the USA
BVHW042259090223
658260BV00005B/144